Thanks for a great
Clambake.

See you next year

[signature]

10/9/00

The Power of the Proclamation

The Power of the Proclamation

Meet Mayor David Bentkowski

THE HONORABLE MAYOR DAVID BENTKOWSKI

Visit www.davidbentkowski.com

BENTKOWSKI BOOKS

Published by Bentkowski Books

Publisher's Cataloging-In-Publication Data
(Prepared by The Donohue Group, Inc.)

Bentkowski, David.   The power of the proclamation / David Bentkowski. -- 1st ed.
   p. :ill. ; cm.

  ISBN: 978-0-9842580-0-0

1. Bentkowski, David. 2. Mayors--Ohio--Seven Hills (Cuyahoga County)--Biography. 3. Seven Hills (Cuyahoga County, Ohio)--Biography. 4. Seven Hills (Cuyahoga County, Ohio)--Politics and government. 5. Celebrities--Anecdotes. I. Title.

F499.S48 B46 2010
977.1/31/092 B   2009937540

First Edition
Printed in the United States of America

09 08 07   10 9 8 7 6 5 4 3 2 1

Dedicated with love to:
My grandmother, Mollie,
My mother, Barbara,
My father, Victor,
the beautiful people of Seven Hills, Ohio

Special thanks to:
Omarosa
Lila Ansley
Karen Miller
Brooke Willis
Christine Riccardi-Victor

WARNING AND DISCLAIMER

This book is a collection of actual events involving Mayor David Bentkowski. The people mentioned in the book are only mentioned because they were part of a public event, they are newsworthy public figures in that they had interaction with Mayor David Bentkowski, and their exclusion would alter the accuracy of the event as it pertains to Mayor David Bentkowski and the telling of his story.

The inclusion of various people in this book does not mean they support, endorse or in any other way approve of this book. The book is subjective and is meant to reflect a series of events as remembered by Mayor David Bentkowski. It is possible and likely that there were other details that could alter the image or interpretation of a story, but again, the author accepts that, encourages people to contact him with supplemental information that can be made available on-line, and has done his best to accurately tell the stories as he experienced them.

Although much of the book is intended to report various newsworthy events, a lot of it also is intended to be humorous, entertaining, and is presented in a tongue-in-cheek manner. Point being, no one should take any claims in this book too seriously and should not be offended in any way by it. If you are incapable of understanding the above disclaimers, you should not read this book - you should go play canasta at a nursing home.

Contents

The First Proclamation: Howard Stern

It all started with the King of All Media, radio shock jock Howard Stern. I'm a fan of Howard's show and used to listen to him all the time until he went on satellite radio. I'll admit I have been too cheap and lazy to get satellite radio. I'll just get it with my next new car.

One of my favorite things about writing these stories about my celebrity encounters is that there are often many "stories within a story." I've always had a philosophy of just saying yes to any idea or opportunity. It was that saying yes that led to one of the wildest weekends in my life. For the record, I originally wrote and had the idea about always saying yes long before the Jim Carrey movie *Yes, Man* was released in theaters.

The first job I had while in law school was for G.E.M. Testing & Engineering Labs, rehabilitating "Brownfields" in Cleveland, Ohio. Yes, yes, yes how noble of me. My boss was a quirky, brilliant, Jewish man named Barry A. Cik. See, he always wanted his middle initial included: I told you he was quirky. I think the world of Barry, and I owe a lot to him. Barry and I both straddle that thin line between genius and insanity. Barry was in Mensa, a very accomplished musician and orchestra leader until a tragic vehicle accident killed some of his buddies after a gig. Barry was an engineer and expert on technical issues. He was ridiculously smart with an equally active desire to create. As for me, I was a talker and a face-guy. Barry hired me to do his public relations and promote the company to local bankers, lawyers, and other boring people.

One of Barry's greatest qualities was he could care less about micromanaging people. No exaggeration, I'd be lucky to see him in the office once a month. The employee's goal was to get the work done, so no one cared what was done otherwise. The office was filled with great people – "manly men" who could scratch themselves and not apologize to anyone. Dave Jilbert, Jim Minut, Chuck Virtosnik, and a cast of others, and some scary Russian guy who never talked to anyone joined me in running the company. I was nice to the foreign guy just in case he went KGB on everyone. We came and went as we pleased, would take two-hour lunches to complain about the Cleveland Indians, would disappear for days if the weather was nice, and almost every morning, listened to *The Howard Stern Show* in the office.

Before anyone shames my work ethic, I have to stress that the work produced by this group was the best. It was always done on time, and everyone would make sure to finish his assignments to keep the Gravy Leisure Train rolling along. It was easily the best place someone could ever work, and it spoiled me for future jobs.

Barry was such a good guy; I remember I was so tired from studying at law school that I couldn't stay awake and fell asleep face down on my desk. Barry came into the office, and I woke up with him and Dave standing in front of me laughing because when I lifted my head up, my face was covered in sleep lines from my sweater and watch.

Barry always had many crazy projects in the works, all neatly sorted (in large Ziploc® bags), covering multiple large tables. The bags would have notes, papers, and objects of whatever related to the idea in Barry's head. I would look at the table and see a bag with a doll and a piece of cotton and think, "What could that possibly be?" The idea in that bag: Barry now runs a successful baby-mattress company in his spare time.

Barry A. Cik, this incredibly talented engineer, and one of the most gifted engineers in Ohio, ran G.E.M. Testing & Engineering with his equally talented wife Regina almost as something that had to be done to pay the bills. It seemed they would much rather spend their time on more creative projects.

One of those "creative" projects was their son, Jeff.

Jeff is the Jewish singing sensation Yehuda! It's not a typo – the "!" is officially part of the name, but I will leave it off going forward because my spell check is lighting up like a Christmas tree. Yehuda might not mean a lot to you, but to thousands of Orthodox Jews across the country, Yehuda is the most exciting thing since matzo ball soup. Yehuda was and is a star. He was clearly talented, young, handsome, and exciting; well, as exciting as someone could be singing traditional Jewish songs. Barry would travel the country with Yehuda and help when he would perform concerts for thousands of fans. Many churches have tried to get more young people involved

Mayor David Bentkowski and his friend, Jewish singing sensation Yehuda!

in recent years. I saw a teen band play "Amazing Grace" with an electric guitar. Well, Barry and Yehuda were way ahead of their time doing this "hip" religious music back in 1997 when I was with them.

A Yehuda concert included smoke machines, hi-tech lights like strobes, lasers, and any other new thing Barry could buy from an *Oriental Trading* catalog. All of these gadgets were controlled and programmed to run "beat by beat" in unison with the music of Yehuda and it was all run on a single computer. Barry was a great P.T. Barnum. He would sternly caution the audience before the show, via the public address system, that there would be "pyrotechnics and strobe lighting" and that guests assumed all risks. The first time I heard him announce this I thought to myself, "I'm about to see some crazy shit happen." Part of it was overselling the drama. The other part was making sure no one tried to sue.

Remember how I said I always say yes to any opportunity? Barry walked into my office one day and said, "Yehuda has a big concert in New York City and I can't go: Can you go and run the computer light-show for him?" I was a capable computer dork who could pull off the assignment. Talk about a great offer! I was getting to go to New York for eight days, get my normal salary, and get to hang out with my friend Yehuda and all of his friends. Sign me up!

I should mention that I am Catholic. I was an altar boy, I cleaned the church before school, I had to wear a shirt and tie in school, I had nuns smack me on a routine basis . . . you name it, I've been there and done it.

What I learned on my first trip to New York with Yehuda was that "Super Jews" – as many of my Orthodox friends affectionately refer to themselves

- start praying on Wednesday and pray until Saturday night. On Saturday night, the reward or conclusion to this week of religious discovery was a Yehuda concert. Best of all, Catholic "goyem" like me were not allowed to hang around and pray with the Jews. Hmm, hanging out in Yehuda's Midtown apartment in New York or hanging out with the Jewish prayer-fest? I was able to forgive the exclusion.

Ironically, a lot of those Jewish girls were smoking hot and hanging out with them could have been fun if it weren't for all those silly Orthodox rules about purity and no sex. Barry and Yehuda are going to yell at me when they read this, and say it can't be true, but I swear, some of those girls gave me the "look." They gave me the look that said, "Hey, Catholic boy, you're taboo . . . I'm here because my parents make me come here . . . and meet me later in the service elevator because I want to rebel." Out of respect to Barry and Yehuda, my official answer is I never encountered that situation. My unofficial answer is, "Jews and Catholics can be close if they try." Here's a pick-up line a goyem can use: "That's not a Z'roa (roasted shank bone) in my pocket!"

So, the whole point of the Barry story was simply to explain how it came to be that little David Bentkowski from Seven Hills, Ohio, was killing time in a sweet New York apartment.

The next thing to know is that little David Bentkowski was Councilman David Bentkowski from Seven Hills. Yes, proving once again anyone can get elected in this great country, I was elected to city council with nearly 75% of the vote in 1995 at the tender age of 23. I was in law school and ran for office because I wanted to help my neighbor, Zora. She was from the old country – not sure which one – but it was old – maybe the Ukraine. Zora, the most harmless granny that one could imagine, never bothered anyone. She worked her whole life and loved living in Seven Hills, easily one of the most beautiful communities in the world. She wanted to spend her "golden years" working in her garden. For the weekend warriors who think they know gardening, they haven't seen anything until they have seen some of the hardcore Poles, Italians, Ukranians, and other old-school Europeans who live in Seven Hills. Zora's backyard looked like Cypress Gardens in Florida. For a mental picture of Zora, just picture some granny holding tomatoes or garlic or some other food on a jar of spaghetti sauce. She could cook and garden as well as anyone. She also befriended my mother, Barbara, a "Martha Stewart of the Midwest" in her own right. Any friend of my mother's is a friend of mine, and the countless plates of lasagna that Zora made for me didn't hurt her cause either. It's idealistic, but if one thinks about running for office and helping people, the Zoras of the world are the reason to do it. She paid her taxes, never complained to City Hall, looked out for her neighbors, and gave out love and friendship to anyone who wanted it.

When Zora did have a problem once and was snubbed by City Hall, it prompted me to run for office and deal with some of those arrogant jerks. I can remember Zora crying to me trying to explain what her problem was in her broken English, and I also can remember my rage at hearing how City Hall workers treated her. I had my cause in life: help those who couldn't help themselves.

The guy I beat was the Council President and had been on council for 10 years. Many years later I talked to him at a meeting, and he discussed how he probably could have done a better job as councilman; but in fairness to him, he was busy and the part-time council job only paid $4,000 a year. It is hard to dump everything into it when it is not what puts food on the family table. When I was elected, I was sworn in by Congressman Dennis Kucinich, the Cleveland Representative who is usually running for the White House. The local paper did the easy story of how I was similar to Kucinich, who had been elected the youngest mayor in Cleveland's history at the age of 31 in the 1970s. The comparison was only partially flattering because Kucinich was the mayor at the helm when Cleveland went into default. I'll give him credit for persevering and convincing people to support him despite his fringe views.

After a successful term, I was re-elected to city council in 1997. One of the things I learned while being on council that first term was that elected officials think very highly of themselves. At almost every dinner or meeting I attended, some official was giving a "proclamation" or "resolution" to someone. In most cities, a proclamation is given out by the mayor. In Seven Hills it officially has no value, has no legal authority, and is basically a fancy piece of paper. A resolution is technically considered official. A city council prepares a resolution similar to the way they prepare a law or legislation. The resolution is introduced at an official meeting and is voted on by the city council. Truth be told, they are both worthless. The resolution, however, supposedly has some type of official quality to it. The proclamation is meant to be something that the mayor quickly can give out at his discretion to anyone he wants, assuming the receiving individual hasn't done something that would cause voter backlash. In other words, I wouldn't give serial killer Jeffrey Dahmer a proclamation, although, believe it or not, I have heard of other mayors giving them to porn stars. I can't imagine what those proclamations say! "Whereas, I do proclaim Destiny Diamonds is hot!" A proclamation is similar to a ceremonial "key to the city." The council resolution usually surfaces when everyone wants "in" on the well-wishing and wants to recognize someone. For example, when the local high school football team wins the state championship, all the council members want to be at the rah-rah event and be able to pander to the parents. These civic leaders need to feel and act important and give the resolution acknowledging this amazing accomplishment. Whenever I hear an official reading such a resolution, I hear comedian Jerry Seinfeld in my mind saying, "Yadda, yadda, yadda."

This is the part where I proudly tell you that, like you, I laugh at the arrogance of some people who think they are so important that they need to proclaim or declare a resolution about something. I am with you on that, which is what makes what I have done with my proclamations so endearing and funny. I realize it's a foolish premise to think anyone gives a hoot about what I want to proclaim, and I have had a blast exploiting the ridiculousness of it. What amazes me, though, is that almost everyone to whom I have given a proclamation has been grateful. It is silly for anyone to think my proclaiming has value, but if it makes people happy to get one, then why not do it? I have given proclamations where it does touch someone, such as giving one to a granny on her 100th birthday; those stories are sweet, as well. I will always try to make someone happy if I can. It's just this amazing dichotomy of something as gimmicky as a proclamation being very valuable and utterly pointless at the same time.

It is funny, but that dichotomy also reflects the job of mayor. In Seven Hills the mayor's job is considered part-time. It pays a whopping $14,000 a year. Again, $14,000 a YEAR! Please buy 10 of these books for your friends and help me. I have lost money on the mayor's gig because I have spent way more on campaigning, giving donations, and attending self-pay events. I have an election committee that accepts donations. When there aren't enough donations to pay for things, I pay for it out of my checkbook. To date, I know this is crazy, but my campaign "war fund" owes me over $30,000. The reality is the fund will never pay this back to me, and it will be forgiven as a bad loan. It seems like everyone asks me for donations and that I am always spending my money. The local high school band wants me to buy a $100 ad in their booster book for uniforms. Instead of boring campaign literature, I create a community newsletter that I personally deliver to 5,200 houses. I pay for this on my own because if I tried to have the city pay for it, campaign opponents would say I was using tax money to promote myself when I just want to update everyone about city business. It costs me $20 for the Rotary lunch, $3 each for campaign signs, and I constantly have employees selling candy and candle junk for their kids at City Hall. It all adds up to a lot of money. If I say no, I am a jerk. I say yes, as often as I can.

What's interesting is that on one side of the coin, I am the mayor of a small town that basically gets dumped on by the locals. Every person who has a problem in the city that can't be fixed gets mad at me. The $14,000 a year salary is a punch-line because the job is a lot of work and takes a ton of time. For someone like me, there is nothing part-time about it. People call me at home 24/7. It is not only my home town, but my parents live just a few streets away from me, so I am trying to make things better. I often find myself spending 40 or 50 or even 60 hours a week on the job. It is a labor of love. So far, it sounds like a terrible gig, huh? A lot of people are unappreciative, and it is a financial loser.

On the flip side, I am the CEO of a community with a $10 million budget. I am in charge of $30 million in fixed assets. I am THE BOSS for nearly 200 employees. I am the only person in the city who hires and fires and who has contract authority. I am the "Top Dog" and what I say is "the final answer." I have seen my actions make a dramatic impact and it makes me work even harder when I see the fruits of my labor take hold and grow. The job has pressure because there are dozens of people who only stay employed if I stay in office. People's livelihoods are on my shoulders.

We abuse our elected officials and many people claim to hate politicians, but I am making positive things happen, and it does have a mystique to it. When people learn I'm the mayor, they do treat me differently. Some call me dirty names and others treat me with respect like I am the President. The public always sees the scandals on television, but the reality is good local public servants do great things every day to make life better for people.

What I witnessed when I first became elected was that most politicians give proclamations or resolutions just to pander for votes. In some cities the mayor generously gives out proclamations. The mayor might have a secretary who searches the papers for information on anniversaries, significant birthdays, or various accomplishments. As for my office, the philosophy is don't look for any to give proactively, but if anyone calls and wants one, sure, we'll give it to him. If someone wants one, then why would I care? If it is a standard one such as for a 100th birthday or a significant accomplishment, then my assistant and friend for 25 years, Chris Matthews, makes it; he is the guy I feel sorry for because it takes up his time. If it's for a band or celebrity, I normally type it up from home because I usually can create it from memory and in a short time. When I bring one I made into the office for a celebrity, Chris stands up and announces, "Hear ye, hear ye, the mayor has something to proclaim" and makes fun of my creation. Then we usually segue into our best Johnnie Childs/Johnnie Cochran impersonations where we try to talk "black" and use a bunch of big words like proclamation, consternation, and precipitation in the same sentence. Holy mackerel, reverend, what the heck did I just say?

Now back to my visit to New York with Yehuda. I drove his music equipment to New York in a huge cargo van from Cleveland. Once there, I picked Yehuda up from his place on 96th and Columbus Avenue. I think this first concert I did was at the Pines Hotel in the Catskills. There was a time in its heyday when the Pines Hotel was the place to be in the Catskills. It had 400 rooms, a ski and golf course, pools, and played host to the likes of Buddy Hackett, Robert Goulet and Tito Puente. It was in 1997 that Yehuda performed. Apparently, the hotel closed up after that year, and I read how squatters, partiers, and all kinds of other vagabonds fleeced and ruined the property. There appears to be some effort underfoot to redevelop it. Once I dropped Yehuda and the equipment off on Wednesday, I had until Saturday night to find adventure in Manhattan and I found it on *The Howard Stern Show*.

Mayor David Bentkowski bumming around New York City.

This trip took place during the Major League baseball playoffs and those loveable losers, my beloved Cleveland Indians, were in the playoffs and should have won the whole championship. Seriously, they lost to the Florida Marlins! But, the connection to Howard Stern started a few weeks earlier. For those who never heard the show, Howard holds court and has an interesting supporting cast that adds a lot. One individual was "Scott the Engineer." On the show, Howard and the gang would love to make bets with each other whenever there was a major sporting event. In the opening round of the baseball playoffs, my Indians were playing those dreaded New York Yankees, the Bronx Bombers, a team with more World Championships than the Indians had players. During their typical betting, Scott wanted to bet that the Yankees would defeat the Indians. Always wanting to stir the pot, Howard called Scott a jinx and said the team he picked always lost. To make things interesting, Howard told Scott that if he bet the Yankees and the Yankees lost, Scott had to walk around Manhattan in a thong and a dunce cap. I hate to tease Scott, but let's just say this isn't a sight a lot of people would want to see. Scott was convinced the Yankees were unbeatable, and he took the bet.

Lo and behold, the Indians won and Scott had to honor his losing bet. This took place when Howard first ran video footage of his show on E! (Entertainment Television). As great as Howard was, pictures often tell the story, and the visual of a fairly heavy Scott walking around New York in a thong and dunce cap was made for television. Like a trooper, though, Scott followed through with his bet. Highlights included burly New Yorkers put-

— 9 —

ting dollar bills in his thong on the street. This type of thing couldn't happen in Seven Hills. In New York, everything was normal.

A couple of weeks later, I was in New York just as the Indians were about to play the Florida Marlins in the World Series. I heard Howard and his gang talk about betting on the game, and on Wednesday afternoon, I had an idea to get on the show. I called Howard's producer, Gary Dell'Abate (Ba-Ba-Booey to fans of the show), and told him, "Hello, I am a councilman from the Cleveland, Ohio, area. I am in town. I would like to present Scott with a commendation for betting on the Yankees. By betting on the Yankees, he jinxed them and made it possible for my Indians to win. In addition to honoring him, I would like to spot him $100 to bet on the Marlins, hoping he jinxes them as well." Friends, the Indians haven't won a World Series since 1948; this was a small price to pay to make our victory happen.

Gary said, "Well, we have a full show tomorrow but it's a good idea. If we need you, we'll call you." Keep in mind, I was in New York for the first time and I was 24 years young. Since Yehuda was off praying in the Catskills, I was in need of something to do. What does that mean? It means I went out and stayed out until about 4:00 a.m. I never thought they were going to call and was just happy to talk to Gary. Lo and behold, at 6:00 a.m. the phone rings. Of course, it could only be one person; it was Gary telling me they were going to put me on the show and I had to be at the station in 30 minutes. It happened so fast. When Gary said I could come on the show, something very important dawned on me: I didn't have a proclamation or a resolution or anything else to give Scott. I was just bluffing and didn't have any office type product with me. I ran to Kinko's, grabbed some fancy paper and a gold seal, and hand-wrote my award in the taxi on the way to the studio. I tried to make it look attractive by using some old trick my mom taught me. I used an index card to guide my pen to create straight lines because there were no paper line guides to follow. The fancy parchment paper was blank. This worked well in theory except because the cab was dark, all of my lines were perfectly straight, but they all trailed straightly down the page in the same manner. My Martha Stewart award project looked like a third-grader made it. I figured if it got me in the door, it was good enough.

As soon as I was buzzed past security, I was whisked into a green waiting room, told to sign a bunch of releases that there was no time to read, and all of a sudden, through the green room speakers, I could hear Howard Stern, the King of All Media, announcing my arrival and calling for me to come into the studio. Don't let anyone fool you; the first time it happens, it is cool - really cool.

Many of my friends would later ask me if I were nervous and the answer is no. I had listened to the show every day for years so I knew all the players and I knew the most important lessons: let Howard tease, don't try to upstage, and make fun of Scott because he was Howard's target. I couldn't have performed better.

Remember, even though I was 24, I still looked like I was about 16. In fact, I pretty much still look the same today as you will see in the pictures. I am 37, and the number one thing people tell me in my community is, "Tell your dad he is doing a good job as mayor." Some age jokes were like batting practice for Howard. Jokes like, "How did you get elected?" and "Did anyone run against you?" were well received. I entered to "Hail to the Chief" – good times. I explained my electoral success by stating that I was the neighborhood paperboy growing up, and I guilted everyone into voting for me. The King laughed. Howard quickly turned his attention to the presentation and making fun of Scott. I explained my appreciation for his jinxing the Yankees. Howard regaled everyone with a funny recap of Scott walking around New York in a thong and laid out the parameters of the new bet. I gave Scott the $100 to bet on the Marlins, hopefully causing the Indians to win. Howard would tease Scott about his weight so I chimed in that if the Indians won the World Series, we would throw a parade in Scott's honor. Everyone laughed when I stated that at the parade, we would put Scott up on ropes like the big floats at the Macy's Parade. I know, cheap, but effective. The Scott joke feeding frenzy was off and running. The segment was funny, no one noticed or cared that my award was handwritten on cheap paper from Kinko's, and I survived an interview with Howard Stern with no permanent damage.

After the segment, the show went into commercial, and everyone was very friendly. Howard, Robin Quivers, and Gary were very gracious with thanks and handshakes. I didn't have a camera and hopefully, Howard, I can revisit to pitch the book and get a picture. History should judge Howard's accomplishments in radio and entertainment kindly because whatever people write or say about him, most of my friends listened to him and thought he was hilarious. Love him or hate him, Howard was an innovator, and for most of the 1990s through today, was considered the best at what he does. To this day, I listen to local radio shows in Cleveland that I like such as *Rover's Morning Glory* and *The Maxwell Show*, and the young radio personalities always acknowledge that Howard was THE guy who made it all happen in that format for everyone else.

I was so excited that I was on Howard's show and hoping that someone had heard it and taped it, that I quickly got into a taxi to hurry back to the apartment to make phone calls. In the cab the driver had Howard on his radio and the guest after me was Tori Spelling of *Beverly Hills 90210* and Spelling "gazillions" fame. This was during her popularity height, and she discussed with Howard how she would like to meet a regular guy. "Uh, hello, regular guy from Ohio here . . . I can help you spend those millions." Oh, well, sometimes fate doesn't give me everything.

There you have it: the first proclamation story even though it wasn't a proclamation. Whether it was a proclamation or not I learned many lessons that day. Lesson 1: It beats me as to why, but people think receiving some type of acknowledgement from an elected official is a big deal. Lesson 2: If I have swagger and confidence and act like a big deal, people will treat me like I am a big deal. The reason this whole thing works for me is because I have the nerve to call up someone, act like I'm important, and convince them that it would be an honor for them or their celebrity clients to meet me. I know, I know, I'm laughing with you. It is obnoxious, ridiculous, and hilarious that it works at the same time. Finally, Lesson 3: If someone is gracious enough to accommodate me or entertain this silly idea, I should go out of my way to make it special for them. In the case of Howard, I was a good guest and a good supporting cast member in the skewering of Scott. For other proclamations, I often gave the celebrity special gifts or personal mementos of Cleveland and Seven Hills. The more I did this, the more I realized I could become semi-famous on my own and use this fame to promote the city I love so much, Seven Hills.

I mentioned that this was one of the craziest weekends ever in my life. The Howard visit was just the start. For those who don't know, the reality for most New Yorkers is that they usually need a roommate in order to be able to afford a decent place to live. People take whoever they can get and if the roommate is not a serial killer, it is usually good enough. Most apartments have two areas that are usually split by a shared living space. The apartments are built in such a way that someone could live with someone for years and barely ever see him. Yehuda's roommate was a normal guy named Kevin. I put that description in about the roommate process because Yehuda is so pious and religious that I wouldn't want anyone to judge him when I reveal what his roommate did. Again, Kevin was a great guy, and while some might find his job offensive, they shouldn't and I don't want to give any imagery that Yehuda in any way hung with a non-religious crowd. A lot of people in New York do not even know what their roommates do for a living. Kevin was a photo archivist by trade. He used to work for one of the big media agencies like the Associated Press or United Press International. He was the guy who would catalog or archive thousands of photographs. I doubt they even have this type of job anymore thanks to computers and the Internet, but back then, he was the guy who knew where to find a picture when needed. His job was eliminated and the only place he could find work doing this kind of archiving was for the porno industry. Believe it or not, every one of those dirty pictures is archived. I don't know why the industry would need to archive pictures of people's "stuff" but apparently it does. The only reason I could figure was in case someone posed when young and then became famous, the photo owners would strike gold. When I teased Kevin about how difficult his job must be, looking at naked pictures all day, he described it as boring. I guess it would get old seeing thousands and thousands of pictures every day. They should give these jobs to 18-year-old boys who would at least stay focused and interested. They would likely work for free. Plus, they probably wouldn't be in an appropriate physical state to walk around the office and socialize.

My story continues when Kevin said he was going to take me to an "industry party" since Yehuda was off praying. Yes, a porn industry party! A big shot at one of the magazines was opening a new restaurant in New York, and he was having a big party to bring his two worlds together. His idea was that having an industry party would bring out a great crowd and get his restaurant off to a good start. I was going to avoid any dish that included the word "glazed." I put on my Value City suit that was five sizes too big and I was ready for action. The restaurant party was packed. Since Kevin essentially worked for all the magazines, he had a lot of hand-shaking and networking to do. He sat me at a table next to a very nice woman from Texas named Ceslie. Being from Ohio, this was all exciting for me. I was still flying high from my Howard Stern visit and now I was at some hip party. I am a people person so I was talking to everyone. At one point I was joined at the table by an attractive woman. Keep in mind, I was a naïve 24-year-old and this woman was probably well into her 30s. My mantra for the night was to act friendly and be appreciative that I was out having a night on the town, so talk to everyone. I was Mr. Social Butterfly. After talking to this woman for about 15 minutes, I saw Kevin across the room looking at me and laughing hysterically with some people. After the woman left, Kevin came over and I asked him why he was laughing. Apparently, the woman I was talking to was a famous dominatrix in New York. I swear it was like talking to a Wall Street executive. She was composed, articulate and intelligent. She even asked for my business card. I was freaking out. I said, "Can you imagine if this woman turns up dead in the Hudson River later and all they find on her is City Councilman David Bentkowski's card? How am I going to explain that one to the voters?" Not once did she reveal her "career" to me and I made Kevin go get my card back from her. If ever I hear about someone's name being in a little black book, I give him the benefit of the doubt because I saw what happened to me. Talk about being out of my element. Coming from Seven Hills, when a woman hits me, yells at me, and makes me stand in a corner, she is called a nun, never a dominatrix.

After my encounter with Ms. Dominatrix, I was a little shaken and went back to talking to Ceslie. I needed to hear her soothing accent. Ohio… Texas … same kind of flavor … hard-working people with good values. Ceslie was a blast. She had a booming laugh and larger-than-life personality. She could be the life of any party. She was good friends with Kevin and knew I was alone, so she dedicated her whole night to keeping me company. The food was great and the conversation better. She had heard me on Howard Stern and we had a great time reliving my encounter. She knew my story but I was in for quite a surprise when I discovered hers. After spending about two-hours together, she finally said to me, "You're so cute, you're so funny, and I love that you are this innocent guy from the Midwest. I am the new Editor in

Chief of *Playgirl* . . . how would you like to be a centerfold?" (Insert scratch of needle sliding off record player and music stopping).

Remember how *Playboy* cleaned up its act and positioned itself as more than just a nudie magazine? Of course, men still bought the magazine to look at the women, but at least it was a pretty good cover to say, "Oh, I read it for its political satire." It just sounded less creepy. Well, Ceslie was a class act with a great business sense; she had just taken over at *Playgirl* and wanted to do the same thing. She was going to make the magazine classier and expand it. She was convinced I would be a hit centerfold. She wanted to run with the whole elected official thing, and I jokingly offered up an idea that if I posed, since I was a politician, I would need some type of "cover" to sell it to my constituents. I offered that she could put an address in my pictures for some charity like breast cancer awareness and as women looked at my pictures, maybe they would donate money. Instead of just skin pictures, maybe the magazine could do a whole write-up about the cause and couch my pictures as "look what David was willing to do to raise money – pose nude." I was years ahead of my time because lots of people pose nude for charity now. Groups like PETA (People for the Ethical Treatment of Animals) have gorgeous models who pose nude saying they would rather be naked than wear fur. As I offered my ideas, I was kidding. Apparently, Ceslie was not because a couple of weeks later, I received a call from Kevin stating that Ceslie was serious. Supposedly she had some ideas to get some corporate sponsors for my fundraising, and I should be getting into shape because pretty soon the whole world was going to see the Big Bentkowski. That's right; that's what I am calling it and I am sticking to it!

At this point, it sunk in that this could be happening and would I be capable of doing it? Part of me said, "Of course, you could do it. Do you know how many times you did it for free in college?" Thank God they did not have camera phones when I was younger. The other side of me said, "There is no way I am doing this. I am an elected official and even more important, my mother would kill me." So, when in doubt, I go to Mom. I figured if I just asked Mom if I should do it, her answer filled with rage would make my decision easy for me. My mother is the most perfect, religious, conservative angel in the world. She makes June Cleaver from *Leave It to Beaver* look like a skank. Mom cleans the church, would cut off her arm to help a stranger, and probably hasn't sinned in decades. She stopped reading my first draft of this book on page two because I used the word "ass" and she hasn't read it since.

There was no doubt in my mind that Mom would get me out of this pickle – or at least from showing my pickle. Once again, I was wrong. "Hey, Mom, it's not for sure, but there is a chance I could pose for *Playgirl* to raise money for charity. What do you think?" Her first answer caused years of damage to my ego: "They really want you?" Her second answer stunned me: "Well, God made your body, and if you can raise a lot of money for charity by taking some tasteful nude pictures, then, of course, you should do it." I couldn't believe it? I had Mom saying "go for it." So, there was a two-week period where I thought I was going to pose for *Playgirl*. I was running three hours a day, doing hundreds of push-ups and sit-ups, and starving myself. Something happened a short time later and Ceslie left the magazine. I don't know whatever happened to my posing, but I never heard from anyone at *Playgirl* ever again. In retrospect, all I can say is I guess I'll never know if I would have done it or not. Okay . . . probably.

After I told Mom that I wasn't going to do it, she just laughed and said, "Did you really think I would let you pose in *Playgirl*?" She was just having some fun with me and got a kick out of my increased workouts. The world was sane again, and everything returned to normal, but I will never forget my week in New York with Howard Stern and the porno industry.

From New York, it's David Bentkowski on *The Late Show with David Letterman?*

Some things always go together in a question format: Coke or Pepsi, Ginger or Mary Ann, and Jay Leno or David Letterman? I was a Letterman guy.

Of course, this discussion has to start with a tribute to the greatest: Johnny Carson. I have liked to entertain and tell stories my whole life, and I can think of two reasons why that is probably so. The first reason is Johnny Carson.

When I was a little kid, I convinced my parents to buy me a five-inch black and white television. Back then, the smaller the screen, the more expensive the television was, and this snazzy portable television was one of my favorite Christmas gifts. Growing up, bedtime was 10:00 p.m. My parents did not know that I would stay up every night until 11:30 p.m. and watch *The Tonight Show with Johnny Carson* on my tiny screen under my covers. Yes, I have vision like Mr. Magoo now. Clear as day, I can remember hearing my dad's footsteps toward my room coming to check on me and me turning off the sound and shoving the television under a pillow. I loved Johnny Carson and loved the way he told stories. Always the entertainer, I would hold court at school the following morning and perform Johnny's monologue. I like that I am all over the place with pop culture. I know all the young stars of today, but I also remember loving Don Rickles, Zsa Zsa Gabor and Jimmy Stewart - thanks to Johnny. The other kids and I wouldn't even understand most of the jokes I was re-telling, but I just loved repeating them and would get laughs just from my presentation. I even put a star on the playground concrete as my standing mark.

On many nights I would stay up to watch David Letterman after Johnny. I do remember the Velcro® wall and Larry "Bud" Melman and early skits featuring Chris Elliot. I thought Letterman was edgy and different and quirky like me. I'm pretty sure I was the only kid staying up past 1:00 a.m. most nights. I could never sleep then and I barely sleep now. I may have been tired because of those shows, but they definitely helped craft my personality and people skills over the years. Someone can be brilliant in academics, but if he is a stiff and can't hold a conversation, then what's the point? Johnny and Dave taught me how to avoid being shy and how to talk to people.

The second reason I like to entertain and tell stories comes from my early days at the Royal Donut on State Road in Parma, Ohio. I know, I know . . . what? When I was in grade school, my family moved from Parma to Seven Hills. My friends thought we were millionaires because Seven Hills was such a gorgeous city and had this amazing reputation. To kids, everything seems so much bigger or so much farther away. After the move I was the only kid from Seven Hills who went to St. Francis de Sales. My house was a 10-minute car ride from the school, but everyone acted like I lived on Pluto. My dad, Vic, worked during the day and my mom worked the second shift to make sure that one parent was always home for my siblings and me. My dad would go to work early so he could be home early to watch us. Royal Donut had an old-style counter with those spinning bar stools, and it had a handful of tables. Since my dad had to be at work by 7:00 a.m. and there were no busses that came out to Seven Hills, my dad would drop me off at the Royal Donut every morning with $1 and I would eat and wait there until the other kids started walking to school about 8:30 a.m. For almost my entire grade school career, I had the same routine. Every morning, with that $1, I would eat a "cherry-charmed" glazed donut – the glazed donut with the pink cherry frosting on top. Also, depending on the time of year, I would drink either chocolate milk or hot chocolate. The same sweet granny would wait on me every day and would keep an eye on me, talk to me, and make sure I went off to school at the right time. Even though people would raise an eyebrow at this today, Parma is still safe, and I would feel comfortable doing this with my kid. Back then, a parent wouldn't think twice about it.

Royal Donut had a regular cast of characters who would come in every day. *The Plain Dealer* newspaper delivery guys would just be finishing their shifts. Yes, I know the joke, but there would be police officers who would come in either after finishing or before starting their shifts. And, there was a group of seniors who would come in every day. Those seniors would sit around and talk politics. I love my seniors more than anything. My community is one of the oldest communities in the state of Ohio. Last election, I received 82% of the vote and my greatest thrill was standing at the polls kissing my seniors as they came out in force to vote for me. Just as for my neighbor, Zora, I would do anything for my seniors. Having said that, my seniors – and most seniors – will probably laugh and admit that they love to bellyache and complain about almost everything. There was a great episode of *The Simpsons* where they had a "Gripe at the Mayor" night and the seniors forced Mayor Joe Quimby to call a new highway the "Matlock Expressway."

Every day I would sit at the counter and listen to these seniors talk about life and government. Like a sponge, I would absorb everything they were saying. I heard every argument about taxes, and pensions, and city services. I would have been a good city council candidate at age 10 – seriously. I still can remember some of their faces and voices in my head, and I would keep track of who would win the various arguments. It helped train me to be a good debater and know how to stress key points and be an effective advocate.

As I said, every day for many years the same sweet granny would wait on me. After grade school I went off to Padua Franciscan High School and the University of Toledo. After I was home and in law school and elected to city council, I went to Royal Donut for the first time in eight years. Most of my family switched parishes and attended St. Columbkille Church close to us in Seven Hills, but my dad still attended St. Francis de Sales; he was active in all kinds of groups and didn't want to leave his buddies.

One Sunday I was going to meet my dad for church at St. Francis. We were going to meet at Royal Donut and I was early. So without even thinking, to kill time, I sat down at the counter and started to read the paper. All of a sudden, without even giving an order, I saw a cherry-charmed donut and cup of chocolate milk being pushed in front of me. I looked up, and with a tear in her eye, my granny waitress said, "I missed you so much and I am so proud of you." I started crying and gave her the biggest hug one could imagine. After eight years . . . EIGHT years, that sweet angel remembered her little David. God, I love my seniors!

I'm not exaggerating when I say if it weren't for watching Johnny and Dave, and listening for years to those people at Royal Donut, I would be a different person and in a different field of work today.

I tell the Johnny and Dave story because in addition to Howard Stern, I had my celebrity encounters with Paul Shaffer, Biff Henderson, and Rupert G. on that first New York trip. These people were supporting cast personalities on *The Late Show with David Letterman*. My meeting had nothing to do with a proclamation, but it was fun just the same. While walking around New York, I went to the Ed Sullivan Theater near Broadway and 53rd hoping to score some tickets to see *The Late Show*. The side building doors opened into a non-descript alley. Every now and then, Dave would use this alley for some entertaining purpose. He dropped things off the roof of the building to see them explode. He had motorcycle guys do stunts in the alley. Once he even challenged my favorite tennis player of all time, John McEnroe, to hit a tennis ball across the alley into an opposite office window. Of course, Johnny Mac did it without a problem.

On this day, I noticed a big moving truck right near the alley studio doors. There were two guys trying to unload a big, heavy couch that they were using on the show that night. Since it didn't look like I was going to get show tickets, I said, "Hey, I'll help you carry that couch inside if you'll let me pretend I am a worker and get me inside to see the studio." One guy laughed at my "creativity" and said, "Why not?" Well, I didn't know it then but I know it now, that the guy was Pat Farmer, who was a stagehand and an important part of the show. Years later, Pat was a familiar sight on the show, and he often participated in skits with Dave. You can't say I don't have moxie!

I helped the guys carry in this couch and they let me stand on the spot where Dave came out to do his monologue. The lights were off and the seats were empty, but I could picture what it was like to come out to a cheering crowd and host the show. What a great feeling!

After I was done helping, I stopped at the famous "Hello, Deli" and met Rupert G. I walked around a little bit more and came back and once again, something was brewing in the alley. The crew was filming a skit involving Paul Shaffer and Biff Henderson. Trivia: Paul Shaffer co-wrote the disco smash "It's Raining Men." Since it was still a couple hours before the main taping at 4:00 p.m., there were not a lot of people around and Pat Farmer

Mayor David Bentkowski and The Late Show's Biff Henderson.

saw me and called me over to meet Paul and Biff. I was able to get a quick picture, but unfortunately, Dave was not in the skit and to this day I have yet to meet him. Years later, I did get tickets to the show and saw an episode with funnyman David Spade, but again, still no "Dave" meeting. Who knows, maybe in the future I will have the chance to make that walk out on stage again, but as Dave's invited guest.

I associated with Dave more than I did with Jay Leno. Don't get me wrong, Jay Leno was funny, but I just always thought Dave was more my style. My brother Mark took me in a blizzard to see Jay Leno perform stand-up comedy at the old Front Row Theater in Ohio. He was hilarious. It was when he would do the joke about his dad throwing the Christmas tree on someone else's yard, and then come home to find out someone had thrown his tree in his yard and then complain about the neighborhood turning bad.

I also related better to Dave because of our relationships with our mothers. Dave's mom was hilarious and a frequent guest. She was as sweet as pie. In fact, she often baked pies on the show. She was like my mother in that she was funny to everyone and didn't understand why. I have done a cable access show with my mother and my friends Matt Fuller and Dan Monroe called *Around Town*, and she was the star. She was all serious as she made recipes, and I joked around the whole time and tried to knock her off focus. She would ignore my jokes or give me a dirty look indicating she was not amused by my antics. Our bond and chemistry was one that could only occur between a mother and son. One time my mother was making chicken and very seriously said, "David, remember, always wash your meat." How could

Mayor David Bentkowski and The Late Show's Paul Shaffer.

I not laugh at that? I was crying in the video trying to stop laughing, and she finally looked at me bewildered with no clue as to what she said that was so funny. I started the show with mom because her holidays and recipes were so over-the-top. I wanted to document all the thoughtful and creative things she did. Her Christmas trees were better than the ones at The White House. Her pierogies were the best I had ever eaten. God forbid if something ever happened to her, I had hundreds of hours of footage that the family and grandkids could use to remember her great love.

I liked to tease her that she was turning into a diva like Diana Ross. When the show started, it was supposed to be "Five Minutes with Mom." Soon, some weeks, she wanted "Twenty Minutes with Mom" and I was waiting for her to make demands for per diem and limo service. She was calling me with show ideas that would be a burden for a network let alone for me. "Uh, mom, I don't have a satellite truck to do a remote from the polka party. Let's not forget we have six people watching us."

Last year, just to experience the process, I filled out the paperwork for Emmy nominations and entered our shows with the National Academy of Television Arts and Sciences. By the grace of God, mom and I were both nominated for a local television Emmy. We lost, ironically, to some show out of Indiana, Letterman's turf. How cool was it that I pulled off this dog and pony show to keep mom active and spend time with her, and she received an Emmy nod? She was so excited. She bought a dress and we went to dinner. For one night, she felt like a movie star.

Mayor David Bentkowski checking out The Toasters ska band.

Over the years, I have appreciated meeting new people and creating new stories. I thought of how classy Johnny Carson was and how much people loved him. I thought of how David Letterman made people laugh and feel better about their day before they went to bed. It didn't take much effort to tell someone a story, or make him laugh, or do a kind gesture for him. Part of writing this book was a similar effort. The more I learned from other people and heard about their lives, the more I realized we were all pretty similar, and there was something to be said about enjoying the journey together.

Reflecting on New York, I'd be remiss if I didn't mention one of my favorite ska bands, The Toasters. I have met them many times since I first wrote about them when I was in college and this mention was just meant to be a "thanks" to them for many great concerts.

"Wouldn't It Be Awesome to Party with George Clinton?"

The years went by and I was happy with my accomplishments as a councilman for my city. I wish people would get involved more in their local governments. My city has 15,000 people so it is not super small yet I am lucky if two people show up at a city meeting. I know people are busy, but local government touches every part of their life. We plow and pave the streets, we pick up the leaves, we provide police and fire protection, we pick up the trash and recyclables, we collect taxes and spend the money . . . the list is long. For most people, their home is their most important investment, so wouldn't it make sense that everyone in a community should be active in the community to enhance and protect that investment? Call me crazy for thinking that way.

I have two best friends. I introduced Chris Matthews already. I met him on the first day of high school at Padua. If I am still around the area when I have kids, I will send my kids to Padua because it was a spectacular school. The friends I made there and the influence it had on my life is hard to quantify. It's been almost 20 years since I graduated and my former English teachers Lila Ansley and Karen Miller were the first persons I called to help me with this book. Padua has produced many successful people including actor Sean Faris from *Never Back Down*; National Hockey League player and my former baseball buddy, Brian Holzinger; Jim Sandusky, the guy who invented Velcro® sandpaper; and countless other collegiate athletes, business owners, community activists, and scientific leaders. I remember how easy college was for me because it was mostly material I had already learned at Padua. It used to be an all-boys school, but thankfully started going co-ed right before I attended. Not that I had a shot with pretty girls like Lisa Leguizamon or Cindy Shumaker, but at least it gave me hope.

The same day I met Chris, I met my other best friend, Joseph Shumay. Like Chris, Joe works with me and the City of Seven Hills as our director of recreation. Notice how I said he works "with" me, instead of for me? Our friendship is more important than affirming the chain of authority. Yes, I hired my friends. Duh, I wanted people I could trust to do a good job around me. Well, Joe was the first "friend" in my group to buy a house. God bless the people of Seven Hills; they first elected me mayor in 2003 when I was still living in my parents' house. Thankfully, I was able to buy a sweet "crib" in 2004. It was a Polish thing . . . we're frugal; we like to pay cash for our houses. Plus, I was close with my parents and I enjoyed spending time with them because I could have lost them any day. In addition, if I needed privacy, I just did a Bill Clinton/Monica Lewinsky at City Hall. I'm kidding. There are too many people that have master keys to even think about trying that at the Seven Hills City Hall.

In the early 2000's my group of friends had a daily routine. We worked and then all would go to Joe's house. A couple people in the group smoked so we would hang out in the attic because Joe and his wife, Missy, had just remodeled their house. It was a peaked attic, but a giant table fit just right and almost every day there was 10 of us hanging out playing cards, the board game RISK, and watching television after work. We were the original *That 70's Show* smoking circle. The cards we played were Texas Hold 'em just as it became huge. Feel free to call us nerds, but we also all loved the game RISK. We played world domination, and it was amazing that friendships survived. The concept of RISK world domination was that a player only won when he took over the whole world. The games could take days because if one person was winning, everyone turned on him, and he would go from almost having it all to having nothing. I'll never forget the time our friend, Marty Noton, owned about 98% of the map and about an hour later was eliminated. It was in the middle of a blizzard about 4:00 a.m., and he was so mad he threw the board game off the table and drove home. We were all laughing too hard to care. Marty was affectionately called "Party Marty" and because he was always the life of the party, it made his serious outburst funnier. Let me give interested nerds the secret to winning RISK when playing world domination: control North America. It was the same reason why the good old U.S. of A. kicked ass. Whoever controlled North America could only be attacked from three locations: Asia, Greenland, and South America. The key was to protect those borders and keep adding a lot of armies every turn. Conversely, just like history, trying to own Europe was a waste because a player could get attacked from too many places (just ask the Poles and British) and Asia was too big and risked too many armies trying to control it.

As a respected elected official, I always caution children about the dangers of drugs. However, the truth was we all knew some potheads and if a couple of the characters that played RISK with us occasionally showed up high, it usually just made the game more entertaining. Plus, those people usually lost first and went and made us all food. As adults over the age of 21, let's just say we all had our drink of choice. If someone was snowed in during a Cleveland blizzard and playing RISK for 86 straight hours, trust me, he would get liquored up, also. Find a sitter one weekend, call some dear friends, and try it; super fun!

In the attic was a cheap boombox. Kids, a boombox was a big radio that originally had a cassette player and then got really cool when it played CD's. As funny as it sounds, it was cool for about a week in 1987 for big black guys to walk around town holding giant boomboxes up to their ears blasting music. Check out LL Cool J and the song "Radio" as a point of reference. No, I am not telling you what an 8-Track is or a record player! In Joe's attic we had a collection of CD's that were played countless times. Everyone's favorite CD was a funky collection that had classics like Young MC's "Bust a Move" and Rob Base's "It Takes Two." The granddaddy of them all, though . . . the song that "tore the roof off the mutha" every single time was . . . drum roll . . . "Flashlight" by George Clinton and Parliament Funkadelic. I have heard that song around 5,000,000 times and to this day when I hear it, I love it. When "Flashlight" played, as George would say, "If you ain't gonna get it on, then take yo dead ass home."

Before I tell the story of meeting George Clinton, he deserves a large amount of predicating. Make no mistake about it - hands down, not even close, George Clinton and P-Funk is my favorite band in the world. If I had to choose between listening to just P-Funk or all other music without P-Funk for the rest of my life, I would choose P-Funk. I have been to 100 concerts, and of those probably 50 of them were P-Funk. If I had to list my top 50 concerts of all time, P-Funk would be 40 of them. See my point? I love P-Funk the way New York Mets fans love Bill Buckner. For people who might not know much about George Clinton and P-Funk (old white honkeys), he is truly music royalty. He is considered the Godfather of Funk. He has been doing music for 50 years. He started in a doo-wop group but came to fame in the 1970's with Parliament and later Funkadelic.

Back in the 1970's most cities were lucky to have one "black" station. Back then, when an artist made a record, the whole record was something. Today, these little teeny-boppers make one hit and are famous for about 10 minutes before the business spits them up and moves onto the next no talent, processed, studio created sensation. I love talking to old black friends who talk about how back in the day, they would go to a party on a Friday night and someone would put on a Parliament record. The whole record would play. As my friend Clark Byers said about "Flashlight," - "that song was the joint." I'm from Seven Hills, but I'm pretty sure that "the joint" means it was good.

What was even more amazing about George was that he was a concert visionary. He spent crazy amounts of money on his shows. A concert today is often boring and bands lip sync most of the performance. A P-Funk concert had those bad mamma-jammas sing every word and play every note. They sounded even better live, and they played for three, four, even five hours. "Ain't no party like a P-Funk party cuz a P-Funk party don't stop." There are old concert videos available from when George would have a "Mothership" with flames and explosions land from the rafters of an arena and he would emerge. I am pretty sure fans won't be seeing a spaceship land any time soon at a Jonas Brothers concert.

I mention, "Mothership?" Well, one of George's many story lines was that he came from another galaxy to beam funk into the butts of people who wouldn't dance. Another brilliant creation of George's was to have multiple stage and song personas. Dr. Funkenstein, the Atomic Dog, the Mothership – George was always giving new characters and songs to his following to keep it interesting. I went to a P-Funk concert once and saw two little white kids in grade school dressed up in full spaceship regalia. Ten years later, I talked to this guy at a P-Funk concert and I told him about those kids I saw. He laughed and revealed that he was one of them. Godspeed, Captain Nathan Lear. The closest modern comparison I could make was how Jimmy

Mayor David Bentkowski with legendary hip-hop group De La Soul. Check out the sweet P-Funk shirt on the Mayor.

Buffet, the Mayor of Margaritaville, shrewdly created synergy between his songs, his lifestyle, his business interests, and his concerts. At Buffett concerts, there were people dressed like sharks, and pirates, and sailors and even cheeseburgers. Fins up, fellow Parrotheads, Mayor David was a Buffett fan all the way back in high school.

George Clinton and Parliament Funkadelic were inducted into the Rock and Roll Hall of Fame in Cleveland. These legends have earned their place. It has brought me great joy to turn on new listeners to their music. Kids today probably have no idea that most of the hip-hop songs they have heard sample George. "To the window, to the wall, to the sweat drip down my . . ." – sorry kids, Usher's "Yeah" wasn't where that originated; it was from George. Whether it was performed by Snoop Dogg, De La Soul, Ice Cube, or hundreds of others, almost all funk and hip hop songs could somehow trace their roots back to the mind of George Clinton. Ya Dig! Recently, I was lucky enough to catch the De La Soul concert celebrating 20 years for the album "3 Feet High and Rising." They were awesome and in tribute to George, I wore my P-Funk shirt in the picture. De La Soul used the rift from P-Funk's "Knee Deep" in their smash 'Me, Myself and I.'

I'll talk about George and the rest of the band many times in this book. They were a recurring adventure and the source of countless good times. But, let's start with the all-important beginning of this musical love affair.

I was sitting in the attic playing cards with Joe and his wife Missy. She was just as awesome as Joe, and if ever two soul-mates found each other, it was these two because they couldn't be more perfectly matched. I recently told them to stop having kids so they could be fun again. I bought Joe condoms for Christmas last year, yet they had their fifth child. Joe, we got it, your seed works. Stop having kids and watch Cinemax instead. Missy was the coolest wife anyone could want. We were rocking out to P-Funk, perhaps with a couple of drinks in us, when Missy said, "Could you imagine partying with George Clinton?" As I thought about this question, I found myself saying, "You bet I would party with George Clinton." Asking me if I wanted to party with George Clinton was like asking a Catholic if he wanted to pray with the Pope. A few weeks later, George happened to be in town at the historic Cleveland Agora on Euclid Avenue. It was the first time the three of us went to P-Funk together. We sat in the balcony and I saw something I wouldn't have believed if I didn't see it with my own eyes. During the song, "Atomic Dog," George brought women from the crowd on stage to dance with him. While dancing, a black woman took out her weave and used it to beat a very private part of her body. Now, I'm white and 37 and I still don't understand what that meant, how she did it, or what a weave was! All I knew was that one second she danced with George and had long hair, and 10 seconds later, she had short hair and horsewhipped herself in a place that some refer to as "Happy Land." I would pay money to have a video of the looks on our three faces as we just looked at each other trying to figure out what exactly happened on stage. "P-Funk, uncut funk, the bomb!"

After that concert, our love of P-Funk grew. Every time we went to a new concert I learned more songs and sang more. After five shows, I was a freak fan that couldn't get enough.

I became such a fan of George's that I wanted to do something thoughtful for him. I had so much fun at his concerts that I wanted to think of a way to thank him. So, just out of luck, the next time George came to town, I cleaned my desk and found an old cassette tape of my appearance with Howard Stern. Yes, a friend had taped it. When I saw the tape, it reminded me of the "power" of the proclamation. I thought, "If Howard and Scott liked and were appreciative of that worthless hand-written nonsense I gave them, how would George feel if I created a beautiful one for him?"

I went online and found George's website. It had a contact number for the media and so I called. I explained I was a huge fan and that I wanted to meet George and give him a proclamation. The woman said she would get back to me. A couple of hours later, I received a call from Shonda Clinton, George's granddaughter, better known as Sativa Diva. Sativa was her own talent and during concerts her one song brought down the house. That was what was so great about a P-Funk concert – it seemed like there were 100 people in the band. People were constantly coming and going on-stage and the multiple layers of talent just made it always seem fresh and that something new was happening. Sativa had this cute, angelic face. She had a million-dollar smile, cute cheeks, and perfect skin. During concerts, she took the mic and rapped one of the dirtiest songs ever written. When I saw this little cutie sing such a hardcore song, it just made it stand out that much more. The song was called "Something Stank" and it was a song about smoking weed. The second part of the song, the "hard as steel" part, was basically a tribute to male body parts and how a guy better bring his "A" game if he was going to fool around with Sativa. Once Sativa kicked into gear with the dirty stuff near the end, George grabbed the mic from her hands and shook his head in grandfatherly concern. The fans cheered and Sativa smiled and was done for the night until the next show where this little spark-plug ignited the crowd again.

Sativa called me up and said George would love to meet me and receive the proclamation. We made some small talk and she even gave me her cell phone number and instructions on where to meet the band. This first meeting was going to take place in Columbus. The band was playing there the day before Cleveland, and I wanted to go to both shows. I drove down to Columbus with my friend, Wade Cramer, and met up with my other friend, Tim Maffo, now a brave Cleveland police officer. Tim was in college at Muskingham University, some tiny school in the middle of nowhere, Ohio. He had worked for the city previously as a lifeguard and we played softball together on the world famous "The Casket Store" team. Yes, my softball team was named "The Casket Store." The first year we played, no bar would sponsor us. We sucked. We had a Croatian kid on our team that had only played soccer previously and he would try and kick the softball to stop it. He eventually rolled and broke his ankle – go figure. Our coach and friend Mario Pettiti convinced the owner of a local funeral supply store to pay our sponsorship fee. Believe it or not, the gimmick worked for this guy. The name was so bizarre for a softball team that it was celebrated in the community. Every player in the league laughed about and knew "The Casket Store" team. As boys are prone to do, we created a unity cheer. During games, often at key moments, random players or fans would yell out "Casket" and it was followed by a thunderous "Store" from everyone else. It sounds silly, but the chant of "Casket . . . Store" dominated the fields every summer. If I walked around town with my jersey on, countless people would comment or acknowledge the world famous, "The Casket Store" team. Mario once asked the owner if he ever heard back from customers about the team. He smiled and said, "A lot of people tell me they see you guys in bars." Over the years, we got better and in 2007 we won the entire division and playoffs. The seven-foot-tall championship trophy was displayed next to – what else – a casket – at the store. "The Casket Store" Hall of Fame includes players Tim, Anthony Cole, Brad Cochran, Doug Phillips, Doug Myers, Chad Wilson, Dominic Sbroglia, Carl Sullivan, Mario and his brother, Chris, Tim Slovensky, and, of course, David Bentkowski. I have played shortstop, second base, and currently pitch.

When I was meeting someone backstage, I always bought my tickets separately and never hoped for or relied on free passes. The people I gave proclamations to were bands that I wanted to see in concert so I always personally bought my tickets way in advance because I didn't want to risk not seeing the show. The show could sell out or I hated sitting in nosebleed seats, so I got my tickets the day they went on sale. The meet and greet or proclamation presentation was one event and then going to the show was a separate event. Most of these meetings and presentations were confirmed the day of the show so I always bought my tickets to see the show, and if by chance the meet and greet happened it

From left to right, Brad Cochran, Mayor David Bentkowski, Tim Maffo, Anthony Cole (back) and Dominic Sbroglia. Yes, the team is really called The Casket Store.

— 32 —

was just icing on the cake. If the meet and greet was not happening, I didn't want to also miss the concert.

The funniest thing about trying to meet up with P-Funk was that, well, let's just say the various members of P-Funk weren't the most organized. Some might allege that for many of the band members, the time was always 4:20 p.m. A nephew or neighbor kid who always has red eyes and loves Bob Marley music can explain that for the confused. I witnessed all kinds of funny stories from several of my meetings with them. I befriended several members of the band and had their cell numbers. I usually went backstage to say some hellos but would rather watch the concert from in front of the stage with the crowd. Most P-Funk shows were general admission and I got there as early as I had to in order to stand in the front row. There was one member of the band – I won't say his name so as not to embarrass him – who was usually so high, I had to call him four or five times on his cell for him to come to the back door to let me in the venue. Ring . . . "Hello?" . . . "Hey, it's Mayor David, can you come get me in back?" . . . "Oh, sure, Mayor David, I'm coming now." Ten minutes later . . . Ring . . . "Hello?" . . . "Yeah, it's Mayor David again . . . I'm still waiting in back." . . . "Oh, I'm sorry Mayor David, I knew I was forgetting something." . . . Ten minutes later . . . Ring . . . "Hello?" . . . "Hey, it's Mayor David again." . . . "Who? Oh, Mayor David. What's happening, Mayor David? How you been?" . . . "I'm good . . . I'm still standing in back waiting for you." . . . "You're coming to the show tonight, Mayor David? . . . that's great . . . do you want to come visit backstage?" . . . "Yes, remember . . . that's why I am standing outside . . . you were going to come get me, remember?" . . . "Oh, yeah, Mayor David, I forgot . . . I'm coming now."

This exchange usually went back and forth for about a half-hour. I kid you not! One time I was standing by the back door and there was a $7-an-hour rent-a-cop guarding the access like he was watching the Berlin Wall. P-Funk was not Justin Timberlake. There were no screaming 16-year-olds yearning to touch the band members. The people coming and going backstage at P-Funk were pretty much family and friends. I wanted to tell this cop, "Look, I'm a grown man; do I look like I am trying to bum-rush George Clinton just to meet him? What am I going to do, cut George's hair and sell it on eBay?" The members of P-Funk didn't seem to mind the people coming and going. Heck, they would probably let me drive the tour bus if I wanted. Remember, there were a lot of people on 4:20 p.m. time. Anyway, the cop wasn't budging and finally after calling and calling, the back stage door opened and my hook-up stood like a vision and inched closer to finishing his assignment. As he stood on the steps, I could see the pain in his face as he struggled to remember why he went outside. From about 100 feet away, I yelled his name – he smiled and remembered why he went outside – waved okay to the guard to let me in – and went back inside. Vintage P-Funk!

I tell this story because I had to put some work into meeting Sativa the first time as well. Obviously, George was not the contact. Quite frankly, I wouldn't want to bother George and calling young Sativa and explaining things to her was just easier for all parties involved. What was funny about going backstage was that many times I had to make it happen on my own. I understood and appreciated what an intrusion I was for some of these people. For a pop artist like Justin Timberlake, there were handlers and radio station people, and managers. For P-Funk, I was calling P-Funk. I called Sativa and said, "Okay, I'm here ready to give the proclamation." She was super sweet and talked to me like we had been best friends for 20 years. She said, "Okay, Mayor David, we are back on the busses; come on back." In a P-Funk world, that directive made sense – just come on back. Unfortunately, on planet earth, people like Sativa forget that there were people called "security." She said, "Okay, see you soon" and then hung up the phone. How the heck was I going to see her soon? No instructions, no special passes, no handler . . . just a "come on back." So, with all the swagger and bull we could muster, Wade, Tim and I just walked on back. We decided that if we acted like we belonged, others would think we did. We just walked back . . . a guard asked what we were doing . . . I dropped names like Nipsey Russell dropped rhymes . . . and got us to the busses. I knocked on the bus door and no one answered. The driver was asleep at the wheel. I knocked harder, and he was out cold not even flinching. After a few minutes, singer Kendra Foster came out of the bus. I told her who I was and she said, "Oh, they're expecting you, just go sit in front." Kendra was very talented and also ignited the crowd when she sang "Bounce to This." One of George's most brilliant moves was to showcase these various up-and-comers.

A band bus was pretty much a spruced-up Greyhound that had been converted. The front had a little sitting area with two booth seats facing each other with a TV overhead. There was a small kitchen with a microwave and sink. There was a bathroom and most of the rest of the bus was beds. Even though the bus was custom made, it had to suck to travel the country on it. I suspected band members were usually just sleeping from gig to gig. Tim, Wade and I sat on one side of the booths. On the other side of us was an old gentleman who could best be described as a look-a-like for Grady from *Sanford and Son*. It was an incredibly ironic description for him because overhead on the TV was playing – ding, ding, ding – *Sanford and Son*. The guy didn't even wake up when we arrived. Even funnier, on his leg was an open magazine that had about an ounce of weed on it. The three of us were laughing like little kids at the scene. Seeing as how he managed to sleep and not spill any of his weed, one could only conclude that he had obviously done that before in his life. The bus itself reeked of weed and had a permanent "haze" in the air. It reminded me of a *Scooby-Doo* cartoon where it would be so foggy that Scooby would use his nail to cut a circle in the fog in order to see. By the way, Scooby Snacks? Acid stamps! The dog could talk, they were constantly seeing ghosts, and they all had the munchies. Where were the parents? Zoinks! Various members of P-Funk walked back and forth as they came and went on the bus. Everyone said hello, and seemed to know who I was and why I was there waiting. Sativa eventually came out and she was adorable. She was fun, sincere and sweet. One thing I always wanted to stress was that I do appreciate how accommodating and kind almost everyone I have met has been. They do not have to meet with me or other fans, so when they do take time out of their life to do this, I like to give them back a little something. I brought Sativa an Ohio State shirt to wear – she put it on and wore it onstage later that night. I also found at TJ Maxx a great XXXL Cleveland Buckeye jersey. It was from the Negro Baseball League, and I thought it was a perfect gift for George because it was scarlet and gray, Ohio State's colors, and it said both "Cleveland" and the "Buckeyes" on it. Plus, it was of a size that could fit George, a very large man. When George pulled it out of the box and held it up, Tim and Wade both had a look on their faces like, "Oh, my God, did he just give him something that said 'Negro' on it?" White people, it's okay. If it was actually called the Negro Baseball League, white people are allowed to give that word and shirt to a black man. By the way, I have known Tim and Wade forever and they are two of the least racist

The first meeting between Mayor David Bentkowski and George Clinton. Check out the Mayor's watery eyes from being on the P-Funk tour bus.

people I have ever met. I think their look was more one of "Where is David going with this one?" This reminds me of some other interesting and ironic psychological tendencies. The frat guy who gay-bashes, was a tough wrestler in high school, and brags about all the chicks he bangs? Yep, he is usually a closet homosexual. If the neighbor is a meek, quiet guy who is a loner and loves his turtle? Yep, he could be a serial killer. I'm just saying people are not always how they appear. I love when they interview the neighbors of a serial killer after he is arrested. The neighbors always say something stupid like, "Bob was quiet and kept to himself." No kidding, I would be quiet, too, if I had 55 bodies buried in my basement.

After chatting with Sativa, she found and brought George to us. It was exciting. He was so much fun even just being around him was a good time. The first thing George said to me in his husky drawl was "They told me the mayor was on the bus, so I burned my finger putting out my joint. The last time that happened, Chelsea Clinton was on the bus." I appreciated the consideration and respect, but come on, George, next time smoke away.

The proclamation was printed on a big piece of parchment paper and had green frame matting. I swear, when I handed it to George, I thought he was going to take some weed off his friend's magazine and use the proclamation to make the biggest blunt ever. As Eddie Murphy once joked, "roll it, lick it, and smoke it." George was gracious, fun, and posed for multiple pictures. Check out my eyes in the picture. I look wasted. The half-hour on the bus must have produced one heck of a contact buzz. I would have to believe that someone in P-Funk would have access to some good weed. When someone hangs around P-Funk, the question isn't "Did he inhale?" The question is, "Did he breathe?"

Think about what a crazy scene this must have been. The kid mayor, who barely looks old enough to drink, giving a music legend a proclamation on a bus – and I swear – the sleeping guy with the weed on his leg never woke up or spilled anything.

There are so many layers to a story like this to ponder. I think of George's legacy. He's in his late 60s and he is still touring like crazy and still making people like me happy with his musical gift. I'm sure there is some money to be made, but he wouldn't do it if he didn't love it. He could just phone it in and do certain concerts to make enough dough. Not George and P-Funk – they earn it every night. Many in the band have been with George for decades and they put on the greatest shows. I would love to talk to people like this for an extended period. Why do they do it? Is it the love of the crowd? Is it the money? Is it because it's all they know? My mother retired from a bank after 45 years and just to keep busy, works as a waitress. She is sitting on Fort Knox but she still works. Why? She works because that is how she was raised, and she is a Pollack and that is what we do. It's probably a bunch of reasons for the band members. It must feel great to work with other great talents. There has to be a good feeling knowing they are one of the best. The feeling of knowing they are part of something special. Maybe for some of the older members like Michael Hampton and Gary Shider, there is a mentoring component to all this. Michael Hampton is the greatest guitar player in the world and he is the guy that plays "Maggot Brain." The song is so amazing that classic rock stations across the country play it at midnight every Saturday. It is considered the greatest guitar solo in history. I once saw Gary Shider show up at an outdoor concert in Miami for someone else. There were only 20 people in the crowd. Gary hopped into the crowd and had all 20 people around him and he did a couple of brilliant songs before turning it back over to the other artist. It was only a couple of songs, but anyone there could see that he was a superstar.

Maybe someone taught Michael and Gary and helped them, and there is joy in returning the favor to the young upstarts like Kendra and the amazing siren, Kim Manning. Whatever the reasons, the hope is that everyone knows just how much it is appreciated. I am particularly thrilled that George

On the bus with George Clinton from left to right, Joe Shumay, Mayor David Bentkowski, Chris Matthews (front), Crystal Beaulieu, and George Clinton.

Singer Kim Manning of Parliament Funkadelic with Mayor David Bentkowski in front of B.B. King's in New York.

The great guitar player, Michael Hampton, with Mayor David Bentkowski at Nelson's Ledges Quarry Park. Hampton is from Cleveland and plays the P-Funk classic "Maggot Brain."

Mayor Funkenstein meets Dr. Funkenstein - Mayor David Bentkowski with George Clinton at Nelson's Ledges Quarry Park.

Still funky after all these years, KC of the Sunshine Band with Mayor David Bentkowski at the Cleveland House of Blues.

still tours because the touring is the only way I have been able to bring dozens and dozens of new fans to the music. A CD just doesn't cut it. I force good friends of mine to go to P-Funk concerts with me. For the newbies, they are always a little hesitant. They will say dumb things like, "George Clinton? Isn't that the 'Atomic Dog' guy?" Sure enough, after every concert, those newbies are as big a fan as I am. Giving someone a gift of music is a wonderful thing to do. Music has been a thread of my life. When I hear someone like P-Funk, it just makes life better. Best of all, when I share my loves with my friends and they adopt them, we have even more in common. When I go to P-Funk, there is a pool of dozens of people who may want to go. The concerts have been some of the happiest nights of my life. Thank you, George, Sativa, Michael, Kim, Franky Kash, Gary, Kendra, Belita, Bernie, Gene, Steve, Jerome, Calvin, and all the rest.

Like George Clinton, another funky brother from another booty-shaking galaxy is Harry Wayne Casey, better known as "KC," and the leader of the Sunshine Band. I met KC just days before I submitted this book and his concert performance was a non-stop dance party. KC and the Sunshine Band have been around since 1973 and for nearly two hours they discoed, jammed, and got their funk on to the delight of a packed crowd. KC sang "That's the Way (I Like It)," "(Shake, Shake, Shake,) Shake Your Booty," "I'm Your Boogie Man," "Keep It Comin' Love," "Give It Up," and "Please Don't Go." He said to a young girl in the front row, "You probably have no idea who I am. I was your mother's Justin Timberlake." The crowd cheered and appreciated that KC was still having fun making the fans happy. Young bands can really

The white guys from left to right are Wade Cramer, Chris Matthews, and Mayor David Bentkowski. The black guys are Robert Randolph and the Family Band.

Mayor David Bentkowski and Ivan Neville's Dumpstaphunk at Wilbert's in Cleveland.

learn a lot from showmen like George Clinton and KC. They haven't had much chart success lately, but their concerts are better than the concerts of current stars.

Robert Randolph and the Family Band and Ivan Neville's Dumpsta-phunk are two more great bands. They would proudly claim to be in the P-Funk galaxy and meeting them was like meeting the next generation of talented artists who would carry on the tradition of great live performances and funky music.

Gwen Stefani and Gavin Rossdale:
"Thank you for this award or whatever"

One thing that interests me in meeting celebrities is seeing how they do things. There are two cool things about being backstage. One is the actual chance to meet my idols and talk to them. For an analytical nerd like me, I like to see the behind-the-scenes action. I like to see how many people travel with the band. I like to see the enterprise of the operation. I like to see how the people act. Are they cool and laid-back like P-Funk or is it just business and everyone is doing a job? I gauge and analyze the smallest details because it is a learning opportunity, and I incorporate some lessons into running my city. Who had good workers? Who had a good manager or press person? What business skills can I learn from the way big-time musicians with millions of dollars handle their affairs? Meeting people is great but gaining insight is better. Will this artist stay rich and famous or is he the next MC Hammer, losing millions in a year?

One of the classiest operations I encountered was the one associated with Gwen Stefani. She was the awesome front-woman for the band No Doubt. I love that she is smart and still makes records and tours with No Doubt. I hate it when singers leave a great band to go on their own and they flop. Do solo projects, but don't completely leave the original band. The odds of making it solo were one in a million, so stick with what works. Gwen has had a great solo career as well and that was the tour I saw her on at the Cleveland State University Wolstein Center. Cleveland State's Cleveland-Marshall College of Law was my alma mater – rest in peace, alumnus Tim Russert. Gwen has done some acting and has her own clothing lines. She was married to singer Gavin Rossdale of Bush and she was a mom. She was a brand, a fashion icon and a tremendous success. She has been a winner at everything she has tried, and I can't recall ever hearing anyone say one bad thing about her or reading a negative article about her. This was the type of woman we could all learn from and whoever "handles" her knows what he/she is doing. In addition to being the mayor and a lawyer by trade, I have spent a lot of my career handling media and public relations for corporate clients. I have had the great pleasure of working with firms like The Direct Impact Company, Qorvis Communications, Edelman Public Relations, Burson-Marsteller, Direct Design Communications, Tactical Outreach, Dittus Communications, On-Point Advocacy and many other powerful Washington and New York firms. These firms do for politics and business what firms like Creative Artists does for entertainers. Some may handle entertainers as well, but I have never worked in that capacity, so I am not sure. What I do know is that with my background, if I were a famous celebrity, I would handle things in a manner similar to the way Gwen Stefani and her team does. The word that comes to mind is precision.

I called Gwen's people and offered a proclamation. They immediately confirmed me and gave me the details to meet Gwen at the meet and greet. For many concerts the meet and greet was where local radio disc jockeys or contest winners got to meet the artist. It can take place backstage or in a designated area. If I were famous, I would be as proactive and gracious with these types of encounters as possible. The reality for the star is that there always are people with special requests or people who want to meet you. In every city I am sure there are rabid fans, contest winners, and kids from the Make a Wish Foundation who want their meet and greet. My philosophy would be just to accept this and have one well-orchestrated gathering, just like Gwen did. If done the right way, the artist shows up for 10 minutes and everyone walks away happy. This is a great way to keep the promotion wheels turning. Gwen should want to meet the disc jockeys on the radio who play her music and then will talk about how great she was to meet. Gwen should want to meet little Tommy Tonsillitis – the paper could pick up on it and discuss how gracious she was with the sick and needy. Gwen should also want to take a picture with as many fans as possible because, like me, they were going to show the picture to everyone they know and talk about how pretty and cool she was in person. You get the idea – an artist should turn it into a positive "must-do" instead of acting like a fool and running the risk of alienating people. Fans want to rally behind good people.

For Gwen Stefani, her people handled all arrangements. They worked with the radio stations and the charities and people like me. They had everything in place first so when the calls start coming in, they were ready to go. When I called, I was green-lighted immediately and they had specific instructions on where I should go. Once at CSU, we were taken to a banquet-type room that was part of the facility. It was large . . . it was carpeted . . . it was private and secure . . . and it was decorated in typical Gwen style just for the meet and greet. This particular *Harajuku Lovers Tour* of Gwen's had an Asian theme to it and the room incorporated Asian sheets and rugs and backdrops. In typical "Gwen attention-to-detail" style, she decorated the room for the meeting to compliment the imagery of her tour. She even had incense candles burning and the room had a warm glow/vibe to it. Wasn't it smarter to do it like this than have a bunch of people crammed backstage messing with equipment and bothering the band during the show? By doing it this way, she also was able to accommodate a huge crowd. This event had about 100 people in attendance. Of all the ones I had been to, it was easily the largest. Once in the room, the biggest security guy I ever saw in my life came in and laid out the rules. Having a guy like this was a good idea because there was not anyone in the room who wasn't going to listen to him. Fans were not allowed to take pictures of Gwen with their own camera. Luckily, I had a friend who worked for CSU and he snapped an extra picture for me in addition to the official one. A professional photographer was on hand to take the photograph of each fan with Gwen. This was smart. If only a pro was taking the photos, the pictures were going to look great. Further, they were made available online for free for fans in digital form on a chosen website. It could have been the radio station's website (great cross-promotion) or a site promoting Gwen. The only thing I would do differently would be to sell the pictures to the fans, because most people would pay anything to have proof of their celebrity encounter. At a minimum, I would sell them for $10 each and donate the money to a local charity. See how good I am at this stuff? I don't know if Gwen did it, but in theory she could have reviewed the pictures and nixed any she didn't like before they were put online. By using only the one photographer, she limited the number of ugly pictures. If I were famous, I wouldn't want some fan shoving a camera in my face and photographing me at a bad angle or snapping the top of my head or while I was blinking and making a face. In the case of Gwen Stefani, everyone walked away with a picture of her looking like a million bucks.

Once everyone was lined up, Gwen came in, worked quickly through the line once saying hello to everyone. She had a Sharpie marker to sign autographs. She fulfilled every request and she gave everyone enough attention and interest to make them feel special. She would be a great politician. After she went through the line, it was time for the photos. She took about 100 pictures in five minutes. If an artist took 100 pictures with people fumbling and stumbling backstage with their own cameras, it would take an hour. It was very impressive to see her execute. She was joined by her dancers who were fully costumed – again, reaffirming the image she wanted. Also, a good handler should walk before the artist on the line. For Gwen, when she got to me in the line, she had someone tell her who I was and the purpose of my visit. The introduction was very much like Queen Elizabeth being introduced to the President. As a politician, I am pretty good at making someone I just met feel at ease. For many though, especially an excited fan, it can be awkward, so having someone there handling the introductions made it more enjoyable for everyone.

The whole thing took about 15 minutes. Everyone walked away with a great encounter and could easily retrieve their professional quality digital photo for free online. Best of all for Gwen, these people all went back to their seats to enjoy the concert, and Gwen had a clear backstage, not dealing with anyone. It was just the smartest way to deal with the reality that meeting fans was part of the gig.

My encounter with Gwen was a good one. It gave me and my friends a great line that we jokingly use whenever we discuss the "power" of the proclamation. After I gave Gwen the proclamation, she looked at it and said, "Thank you for this award or whatever." Wasn't that awesome? The proclamation was described as a "whatever." Gwen's right – what the heck was a proclamation? It was a "whatever" and I understand that. That's the joke. Who cares . . . it worked and I'm running with it. Whenever I tell Chris or Joe or some other inner circle friend that I am trying to meet someone new, they will say, "It's time to give another whatever." As I have said before, I know and appreciate that it is unbelievably ridiculous that my "proclaimed" words work as a magic key to gain me access to meeting stars like Gwen.

Mayor David Bentkowski, Crystal Beaulieu and Gwen Stefani.

The humor of this fact, and the stories that document it, are the very purpose of this book. So thanks, Gwen, and thanks for being a great story in my book or "whatever" this is. Ironically, even though the proclamation was just a "whatever" that I first used to meet George Clinton, my objective immediately changed. I realized quickly that this celebrity access could be a great thing. I realized that celebrity encounters would be good publicity for my city. I'll talk more about this later, but once I knew what I had, I knew I would use these encounters and proclamation presentations to promote my city and develop relationships that could help my city.

Joining me at my meeting with Gwen was a beautiful girl named Crystal. She was my first real love. We dated for three years, and she will always hold a special place in my heart. It used to make me so happy to see her get excited about things like meeting Gwen. Her big smile was more fun than the concert. During the time we dated, she was a star of her own. Everywhere we went people treated us like we were Gwen and Gavin. At political events, people talked about us like we were a loving couple like Ronald and Nancy Reagan. If we went dancing in Cleveland's Warehouse District, strangers would come up to us and tell us we looked like movie stars and that we were beautiful together. I'm sure they were really commenting on how beautiful Crystal was, but it was thoughtful to be included. Crystal and her friend, country singer Sarah Marie Blanton, even went on-stage once and danced with George Clinton during the "Atomic Dog" portion of the show. Much like Gwen, Crystal was all about fashion, and the red boa Gwen was wearing in our picture was a gift from Crystal. The two were cut from the same

Gavin Rossdale of Bush and solo fame with Mayor David Bentkowski.

cloth and could be best friends if they hung out together. Crystal is married and has a beautiful baby boy. I wish her and her family well and thank her for many great memories like our night with Gwen Stefani. Incidentally, Gwen and No Doubt have a ton of great songs, but check out the song titled "Running." Even though I am a guy's guy, the song is so well done and beautiful that I am secure enough in my manhood to admit it is a great tune.

Years after meeting Gwen, I had the chance to meet her husband Gavin Rossdale after his concert. I always liked his music but was pleasantly surprised to see how talented he was as a performer. I guess it made sense. He didn't front a great band like Bush and marry Gwen Stefani because he was a chump. My meeting with him was unplanned as I just happened to bump into him in the alley behind the venue as he was heading to his tour bus. He was gracious and met with fans, and I told him about my meeting with Gwen. If I meet anymore people from their family, they are going to start including me on their Christmas cards.

Nick Lachey and Of a Revolution:
Mr. Nice Guys

Nick Lachey is a nice guy. It shouldn't come as a surprise because he is originally from Cincinnati. Any place that has Ronald Reagan Highway is all right in my book. My best friend from law school, David Eppstein, was also from Cincinnati (Blue Ash). In law school, students were allowed to come to class unprepared just one time. They had to tell the teacher before class that they were using their one "freebie" and that way, he wouldn't call on them. Dave was hilarious. One day, the teacher started class by reading the following note: "Dear Professor, Dave went out yesterday and is not prepared for class today. Please do not call on him ... Signed, Eppstein's Mom." In the 1970s, there was a popular character on *Welcome Back, Kotter* named Juan Eppstein, and he was always giving Mr. Kotter bogus excuse notes signed "Eppstein's mom." Today, Dave is a lobbyist/lawyer in Washington, D.C. He even worked in the U.S. House of Representatives for the Financial Services Committee. Seriously, he is one of the funniest, coolest people in the world, and I would pay money to hear him deal with Washington bureaucrats on a daily basis.

People in Cincinnati are awesome. The city is unique with lots of hills; Kings Island is a blast; The Beast rollercoaster still rocks after all these years; and Cincinnati people love Jimmy Buffett. If I were ever going to relocate, the area would get consideration. A guy like Nick Lachey growing up in Cincinnati is going to be a lot like David Bentkowski growing up in Seven Hills. There are Midwest values, and guys like us like to do the right thing, treat people well, be kind, and basically go through life not bothering anyone. When a good Midwest guy like Nick Lachey succeeds, I can't help but cheer for him and hope it continues for him because it is reassuring to know that good guys can finish first. He's rich, famous, allegedly took Jessica

Simpson's virginity, and dates Vanessa Minillo. If that's not coming in first, it's pretty darn close. He is a good singer and of the boy bands, his group 98 Degrees was pretty good. He did a smart job reinventing himself as a solo artist, and, of course, Nick and Jessica's *Newlyweds* show was a huge hit on MTV. My friends who watched the show always liked Nick. He came off as a kid from our neighborhood. He was someone I could see being friends with and someone just like me. He was close with his brother and family. He liked to camp and chill. And, he seemed down to earth compared to Jessica, who seemed like a handful. He would shake his head at Jessica and her antics the same way every other guy would shake his head.

I would attend a lot of charity events as mayor. One of the things I noticed was that local news hardly ever covered such events. Quite frankly, it is ridiculous how bad local news has gotten over the years. If some dumb athlete shows up and reads a book to kids for five minutes, the local news kisses his butt and gives him a ton of free publicity. These appearances are set up by a team's marketing department and are so orchestrated it makes one want to vomit. Yet, local news plays along and gives them top billing like they cured cancer. Every time they do a story like this in Cleveland, I call up the stations and complain. My other pet peeve is when a local television personality goes to some event and the station gives some nauseating acknowledgement like "Our own Leo Lipshitz was at the cancer benefit for kids tonight – isn't Leo great – look at him enjoying that free dinner – yeah, Leo!" What good does reporting about the event after it happened do for the charity? It doesn't help it raise money or sell tickets. It's all about self-congratulation. No one gives a shit that the sleazy weather guy was there enjoying a cheap date.

Don't get me wrong, there are sports figures and other celebrities who do a lot for charity, and for those stars I do want local news to celebrate their accomplishments. Cleveland Browns wide receiver Braylon Edwards donated $1 million to local schools. Now, that is being generous! When it is obviously an orchestrated publicity grab, I would rather the station focus on the real heroes working behind the scenes. I'm not exaggerating. A lot of the people behind charitable causes are real heroes who are dedicating their lives to helping others. I would go to these events and I would see volunteers who worked on the event for six months and they never get mention. I would go to these amazing events that touched people's lives, and the local news would never cover them unless there was some cross-promotion like an anchor's involvement with the cause.

My good friend Bill Safos used to be a reporter at Channel 3 WKYC/ NBC in Cleveland. He is an excellent reporter and even better person. I told him about what I saw at these charity events, and he did his best to get them covered by the news desk. To its credit, Channel 3 seemed to do more than most stations across the country. Bill always thought I would be great on television. He gave me the "it" speech. He said, "I don't know what 'it' is as far as being good on television, but you have 'it' and should be on air." Thanks, Bill. Your friendship is always appreciated, and I have learned a lot watching you, an ethical reporter. Bill set a meeting where I met with Channel 3 big-wigs to pitch my idea. I wanted to do something dramatic to promote local charities – something that was a campaign that would gain momentum and build over time. I told Channel 3 that I wanted to do a year-long charity promotion effort where every week I would pick a charity event, pre-promote it to help make it a success, and attend the event and participate in it. I would film it and give the great volunteers their moment in the sun during the review. Every week, the goal would be to review one event while previewing an upcoming event. Another key was the fact that I would participate in the event. I figured to keep things interesting, I had to play the fool and be willing to be embarrassed. The idea was that I would run the 10K for cancer, I would bowl with the kids for autism, etc. By participating, there would be great chances for funny videos, and it would make the segments more interesting.

Channel 3 loved the idea except there was a problem: Channel 3's employees were in a union and allegedly the union contract stated that any filming or production work had to be done by union workers. It would have been extremely expensive for Channel 3 to send a union cameraman with me all over town at all kinds of crazy times as I did my charity effort. It just wasn't going to happen. Perhaps this is why people hate unions. Imagine, my noble effort to help 52 great causes was almost dead on arrival because of some stupid union contract. I understand the goal of unions, but there should always be opportunities to do the right thing. In fairness to Channel 3's union, I do not know if that story was true. I do not know if there was an opportunity for the union to waive any contractual rights voluntarily they may have had.

The Channel 3 union could have performed greatly if given the chance. My comments aren't necessarily aimed at them because I don't know for sure if they were the problem or if station management was blowing smoke. What I do know was that it appeared to be a stumbling block that almost side-tracked my noble effort.

Channel 3 ultimately told me I could do my project if I just bought air-time and submitted my segments as commercials. Wasn't that ridiculous? I wanted to profile 52 charities – donate my time, resources, editing, and filming, and I had to come up with a sponsor to pay for the air-time. Trust me, TV time was not cheap to buy. God sends angels every now and then and my TV angel was Tom Goebel of Lakefront Trailways Bus Lines. This great man and family friend donated almost $60,000 to this effort. If it weren't for him, it would have never gotten off the ground. When the initial sponsorship money ran out, I shelled out thousands and thousands of my own money and managed to finish the entire year. Yep, add these thousands onto the $30,000 my campaign already owed me. My "Giving in Good Company" segments made their debut on Channel 3's *Good Company* in January of 2006. The idea was a hit, and week after week the pre-promotion helped the events succeed and the post-event reviews helped the wonderful volunteers be recognized. Every week there was a great story from the various events I attended so don't be surprised if that is my next book. There are some amazing people persevering in the world and also some great volunteers who put others first.

Good Company had four co-hosts: Andrea Vecchio, Michael Cardamone of *Average Joe* fame, Eileen McShea and Cleveland television legend Fred Griffith. Every week I got to know them better during my visits. I wanted the show to do well since I was on it and was willing to help in any way I could. Andrea was one of the show's producers and wanted to get Nick Lachey to come on the show. He was in town as part of a promotional tour with MTV and a local radio station and was apparently not doing any other media. Andrea wanted me to give Nick a proclamation. She was going to go along with me to try to score Nick's only in-town television interview. I figured "why not" for two reasons. First, I researched Nick Lachey and he did a ton of charity work, especially for groups like Big Brothers, Big Sisters, so the proclamation was deserved. Second, I help my friends if I can, and if giving a proclamation helped my friends at the station have a shot at scoring an interview, why wouldn't I want to help them? I made it clear that I was giving Nick the proclamation because he earned it and that I wanted nothing to do with any of the covert television effort. Knowing Nick was from Cincinnati, I knew I had something he would want. Believe it or not, I had an uncle who collected old beer cans. Much to the chagrin of my mother, my dad also kept bags of these old cans in our crawl space. I guess they were cool in their own way. Many of the cans we had were of beers that weren't even made anymore so there was some value to them. We even had a can of Billy Beer – the beer made by former President Jimmy Carter's brother, Billy. What was ironic was that no one in my family even drinks beer. My dad just liked collecting the cans.

I remembered that we had some beer cans that had images of the Cincinnati Reds from their "Big Red Machine" championship teams from the 1970s. I was a huge baseball fan growing up so I remembered we had these cans that had Johnny Bench, Dave Parker, and Dave Concepcion on them. I dug through some bags and sure enough, I found these 30-year-old Cincinnati beer cans. When I met Nick, I gave him the cans and some Cincinnati apparel ($7.99 sweatshirts from Steve & Barry's) and he loved everything. I probably spent about 15 minutes talking to Nick and his people, and he was everything you would expect. He was friendly, laid-back, and un-pretentious; no phoniness in any way. As you can see in the picture, I was the one in a suit and Nick was in the t-shirt and jeans with a University of Cincinnati hat. Andrea did a good job hustling and did talk to Nick personally, but she couldn't get him to go on camera. Apparently, it wasn't his call

Cincinnati's Nick Lachey with Mayor David Bentkowski.

– he had some commitments he had to honor and wasn't allowed to do other interviews. He promised he would visit the show his next time around and he did. He posed for a bunch of pictures, and Andrea was able to show the stills on the program and at least got something on air. While doing *Good Company*, I was able to meet some other celebrities like Tracy Morgan, Dr. Ruth Westheimer, and Cal Ripken Jr. I tell Andrea that I am mad at her because she took a picture of me with Cal and she can't find it. You know how certain people create a buzz? People were very excited to meet Cal Ripken Jr. He could easily run for and win any public office.

There was a follow-up to the Nick Lachey story. He was back in town later in the year to do his concert at Playhouse Square. After I met him the first time, my mother busted my chops because she wanted to meet him. I called Nick's manager and he said he could help me out. He laughed as I explained that it was Mom who wanted to meet Nick this time. I didn't want Nick to think that a grown male was stalking him. What's interesting was that Nick's meet and greet was just as successful as Gwen Stefani's, but it was done almost exactly the opposite. I guess it just goes to show that a star has to pick a style that suits him. As mentioned, I would run my camp exactly like Gwen runs hers. Nick, on the other hand, walked into the basement of this old building. He sat down behind some wobbly table on a metal folding chair. He was in a T-shirt and just started signing away. People snapped pictures, girls swooned, and my mom held up the line telling him how she wanted his brother, Drew, to win on *Dancing with the Stars* – it was total chaos; everyone walked away just as happy as they did with Gwen. I'm not saying they handled it wrong; it was perfect for Nick's laid-back style; but what a contrast.

I would be remiss if I didn't mention the funniest story from my charity effort. I do not know how to swim. I'm not kidding; if I fell in six feet of water, I would drown. I have a nine-foot-deep pool in my house, and like a five-year-old I wear a life-jacket when I go in the water. You are correct in your assumption that wearing a life-jacket while swimming does not get you chicks. One of the charity events that I profiled was the local YMCA. They had a team of girls aged six through 12 who performed a synchronized swimming program. They had a big yearly "showcase" to raise money. In order to keep the segments interesting, I tried to mix up my charity events. I could only cover so many 10Ks or walk-a-thons or wine tastings. The concept of water footage and something fairly unique convinced me to cover the showcase. When I spoke to the coach, I made it very clear that I couldn't swim, and that I was afraid of deep water. I suggested that I would do some filming with the team after their big event and after the fans and parents cleared out of the natatorium. The show finished, the house lights went on, and people started to leave. Just then, someone announced on the speaker, "Okay, everyone, stick around because Mayor David from Channel 3 is going to join the girls and film a segment." I stood poolside not even changed yet and I had about 1,000 eyes on me. I felt the weight of the stares and heard the snickers as I peeled off my shirt and put on my life-jacket. The room was freezing and the water was even worse. I couldn't have had a worse feeling about what would happen next.

The original plan was that I would hop into the water and play the fool while the girls did their routines around me. I kept envisioning Rodney Dangerfield in *Back to School* or a *Saturday Night Live* skit where everyone was doing his routines, and the humor would be how out of place I was. It was going along fine, and the girls had just finished making a circle around me as I floated in the middle of them with my life-jacket. When I first arrived, I was given a special assistant. I'm not sure if she was a contest winner or was a star pupil, but this adorable little girl was to be my helper. She would be next to me in case I needed anything. It was a quasi-honor for her to be given this special assignment. What I am about to explain was probably the funniest video involving me that was ever filmed. After they finished their circle dance around me, I had about 25 girls encircling me and my little helper. Out of nowhere, the coach yelled, "Okay, girls, splash him!" Instantly, 50 little hands splashed water at me. Hello, dumb ass, I am afraid of water. My whole boring life flashed before my eyes. In the video, one could see the look of horror on my face – almost like a slow motion "noooooooooooooo" exiting my mouth. It probably was only a handful of seconds but it seemed like an hour to me. I could not breathe because no matter which way I turned, I was being pelted with water. And now for the hilarious part that will haunt my future political career: at one point in the video, I put my hand on the head of the little girl next to me and dunked her for leverage so I could get out of the water. Of course, it was only funny because no one was injured, but I was freaking out when it happened. I thought I would drown and the only way I could get air and catch a breath was to be higher than the splashing. As I was dunking her, all anyone could see were her little arms and hands waiving in the air from under water. She was flailing around like prey from a Discovery Channel "Shark Week" video. My assistant Chris knew I was afraid of water and couldn't swim. He was filming that day, and the camera was shaking from his laughing which also was readily audible on the tape. Some best friend; I was drowning and he was laughing and having the time of his life. My friends took the video part where I dunked the little girl and edited it on a loop. I have to admit, it was pretty hilarious to watch. Finally, the splashing stopped, and if looks could kill I would have been a mass murderer that day because I never had a more pissed-off-looking face. It may have been a nightmare then, but at least it was a good story. Some day if I run for Congress, I am sure there will be a smear commercial with scary music that says, "David Bentkowski likes to drown children" and then they'll show that video.

The moral of the story is that I should stay out of deep water. I have only told a couple of people this next story, but when I was seven, I was in Fort Lauderdale with my sister's traveling softball team. We were staying at that famous "L" shaped hotel on the beach that was in those Spring Break movies. There was a group of us in the ocean and I wondered off as I was prone to do. I was going as far out as I could in the water and thanks to the sand bars, I was really far away from the shore. Since I couldn't swim, it was fun for me to be able to participate and be in the water like everyone else. Clear as day, I can remember the tide pulling me out suddenly – and I stepped off of a sand bar into deep water. Parents, if your kid is a dumb ass like me and can't swim, explain the concept of sand bars to them before they go in an ocean. As Austin Powers would say, "I could have used the info." I started to panic, splash, and go under. I swear on my life, out of nowhere, I felt an arm grab me. It was a pudgy Indian woman. Think Indian like Taj Mahal, and not like Pocahontas. I have no idea where she came from and I swear there was no one around me. She literally appeared out of thin air. She was smiling at me as she held my arm and paddled me to closer near the beach. I remember that it was completely quiet and the only sound I could hear was a small humming/laughing type of noise she made as she paddled me to safety. As soon as I was in shallow enough water to stand up, she was gone. I promise this is true. The woman was gone!

I am one of the most cynical people in the world. I do not believe any stuff like this. I don't believe in ghosts, or psychics, or reincarnation or aliens or

Ohio favorites O.A.R. (Of a Revolution) with Mayor David Bentkowski at the Hard Rock Café in Cleveland.

anything else that is not mainstream. But, I swear on my life – or the life of my first born – that this story is completely true. Aside from how amazing it was that this happened; how funny is it that apparently my guardian angel is a pudgy Indian woman? She may not have been what I had in mind, but, she got the job done!

One of my most valuable videos was one I filmed of the band O.A.R. (Of a Revolution). The members of this band were arguably some of the most charitable artists in the world. The list of causes they have helped was impressive. They have helped the USO, the National Guard, and THE Ohio State University. I was able to film them at a special charity concert they performed at the Hard Rock Café in Cleveland. It was a great concert to film because they sang just a few feet away from me in the restaurant. O.A.R. was famous for paying its dues and building a huge following over the years through hard work and awesome concert performances. While at Ohio State, the band graduated from fraternity and sorority house concerts to regional tours. The band now tops the charts and even sold out a concert at Madison Square Garden in New York. When I met the band members, I could tell they were appreciative of their good fortune and that was why they were so willing to give back to help others. The future appears to be very bright for O.A.R. and since the members have acted with such class on their way to the top, supporters and even music critics want them to stay there for a long time. Proving that they haven't changed their stripes, the band members recently waited out a two-hour thunderstorm in Chicago and performed a memorable, albeit wet, outdoor concert to appreciative fans.

The Value of a Proclamation? Worthless? Nope, $375. Ozzie Osbourne and Dimmu Borgir

I can prove that my proclamations are not worthless. In fact, they apparently have a going value of $375. I know this because a proclamation that I gave to Ozzie Osbourne recently sold for that amount. It's crazy but true and here's how it happened.

One day Chris Matthews received a call from the Cleveland Film Society. I know, I know, who knew there was such a thing? Apparently, MTV was in town and it was filming segments for Ozzie Osbourne's new show, *Battle for Ozzfest*. This was a reality television show where a bunch of bands sent one of its members on a tour bus crisscrossing the country completing various tasks. The winner and his band would secure a choice performance slot on Ozzie's popular *Ozzfest* tour. For a rock band, playing on *Ozzfest* was huge. Like George Clinton, Ozzie was musical royalty and thanks to *Meet the Osbournes*, one of the world's most beloved patriarchs. MTV had heard I was the young mayor and that I had a television interest and background. Those were all creative ways of CFS saying, "We needed someone crazy enough to entertain MTV and you came to mind." The band kids had a task and the task, involving me, was that they were going to try and secure publicity for a band. The show also featured Sharon Osbourne giving advice and business examples. Sharon was considered one of the most shrewd and brilliant business managers in the music industry. Her acumen was legendary, and she was apparently one of the last people someone would ever want to cross. The various tasks given to the kids were designed to help them prepare for the life of being a rock star. Securing promotion, in this case from me, was a valuable lesson for them and good experience. We received the initial call from the "kids" and were told to treat them how we would treat any other call. It was intended to be an accurate effort on their part to do the work needed to secure the proclamation and meeting with the mayor. There were multiple bands on the official *Ozzfest* lineup, and the kids were supposed to garner publicity for a Norwegian group called Dimmu Borgir. I had never heard of them and neither did anyone else at City Hall. As part of our normal vetting process, we researched the band while creating the proclamation. Thank God we researched Dimmu Borgir! I never like to criticize someone's creativity since I know different folks like different things. I know gangster rap has deep meaning and can be autobiographical. It may not be my thing, but I can understand how it can be personal for an artist.

Well, let's just say Dimmu Borgir's music doesn't reflect the good old wholesome values of Seven Hills and David Bentkowski. Quite frankly, I felt like speeding to church and saying a dozen Rosaries just from visiting their website. I immediately called MTV back and said, "Look, you know I love you, but you are out of your mind if you think I am giving Dimmu Borgir a proclamation." I didn't want to screw over MTV and leave them hanging, but they didn't exactly go out of their way to explain who Dimmu Borgir was and what they sang about, so I wasn't about to be impeached for them either. In the spirit of compromise, I offered to create a proclamation acknowledging Ozzie Osbourne's contributions to music and his vast charity work. Alleged bat-head biting aside, Ozzie was worth a ton of dough, and he apparently was generous with it and helps a lot of causes. Dimmu Borgir, the kids, and the fancy tour bus could come and accept the proclamation on Ozzie's behalf. At least this way MTV could do some filming and hopefully be able to salvage the episode. It was a good compromise and everyone went along with it.

Two funny things happened when the band arrived. My service director Bill Bishilany was a typical dad. He had gone online and researched who the band members were in advance without telling anyone. The band members of Dimmu Borgir had unique names that were new to me. In front of all of us, Bill went down the line and greeted them, "Shagrath, pleasure to see you. Silenoz, welcome to Seven Hills." We all looked at him like, "How the heck do you know these people?" The second funny thing was we

Dimmu Borgir scared everyone at the Seven Hills City Hall including Mayor David Bentkowski.

were all wired with microphones and kept in a room away from the band. The band thought it would be funny to act like they didn't speak English. Unbeknownst to us, our microphones were live and the band could hear everything we said before our meeting. I don't think we were too gossipy, but there had to be some comments from us about "how scary looking" the band was or "where did they find these people?" No hard feelings, guys. It was amazing the comments weren't worse. We staged a fake meeting and ceremony for the cameras, and it likely was a good learning experience for them to see government in action. They were presented with the proclamation for Ozzie and promised to deliver it to him. The kids and the band members were all very nice. Make no mistake about it, their songs and lyrics and points of discussion were highly objectionable to me. It was not the type of thing a Catholic guy from Ohio would listen to – well, at least not this guy. Then again, I just never know why someone does something. Did they sing these songs just to pay the bills and be famous? Did they believe some of this crazy stuff or was this a performance just like an actor didn't really kill people in a movie? Who knows and who cares? People can pick and choose what they like and it is not up to me or anyone else to tell people what they should be listening to, other than P-Funk. After the presentation, the band members revealed that they spoke English, and we all had a good laugh while we tried to remember what bad things we said about them when we thought they couldn't hear us. They posed for pictures and graciously thanked us for helping. It was fun to talk to the kids in the contest. They were giving their all to pursuing their dream of making it so we cheered them on, celebrated their stories, and ran them up to the Seven Hills K-Mart to get some supplies (beer) for the bus. They were the second famous celebrities to visit the Seven Hills K-Mart. About 20 years ago, the one and only Chuck Norris visited that same K-Mart. "Attention K-Mart shoppers; Chuck Norris is giving a blue-light ass whooping in aisle 10." Chuck Norris is so strong his shadow can beat me up. Chuck Norris is cooler than the other side of the pillow. Chuck Norris is so smooth, he makes silk feel like sandpaper. The legend of Chuck Norris grows.

Our portion of the show never made it to air because Dimmu Borgir participated with the kids earlier in the day in a visit to a local radio station. The band visited Cleveland's famous WMMS 100.7, The Buzzard. On air, the band started dropping curse words and the disc jockey immediately kicked them off the show. Those exchanges and the kids "dealing with their client" became the focus of the Cleveland episode and our portion was cut. The lesson was dealing with radio stations and damage control and other issues involving media. I have to admit, I would have probably wagered that Ozzie and Sharon would have never received the proclamation from the kids after this long cross-country road trip of tasks. But, sure enough, when the kids went before Ozzie and Sharon for that episode, they walked in with the proclamation. Viewers could see it on television.

Fast forward a couple of years and I discover that Ozzie and Sharon Osbourne were selling a lot of their personal belongings for a colon cancer charity. The auction would include family cars, furniture, concert memorabilia and costumes. But, most important, there was Lot 158, page 66 of *The Osbourne Collection*, Mayor David Bentkowski's proclamation to Ozzie. Not only did the Osbournes receive the proclamation, they cared for it for several years and kept it and eventually put it up for sale with their other offerings. How cool is that? I would assume it was Sharon's idea and just another example of Sharon Osbourne's business brilliance to take this "stuff" and do something grand with it. The auction was conducted by Julien's Auctions and raised nearly $1 million. The winning bidder paid $375 for the proclamation that I gave Ozzie. The auction produced an official preview book; I bought one of the books, and it sits on my coffee table and makes for a great story.

The proclamation cost $6 to make and sold for $375. Clearly, the fact that it was "official" Osbourne memorabilia helped its total, but it just gave me a great idea to sell proclamations for charity. Keep an eye on this book's website in the future for info on how I'll do this. By law, I can't accept the money personally for creating a proclamation, but I am going to let people buy a David Bentkowski/Seven Hills proclamation and the money will go to a local charity. Buyers can give one for a birthday, graduation, or any other non-offensive reason. Hey, don't laugh; there are thousands of people that buy the naming rights to stars in outer space. At least my proclamations will be personal and the money will go to a great cause.

This Ozzie experience holds many great lessons. For starters, it was the first time I noticed the expense and production that goes into producing a television show. MTV had six cameramen, multiple sound and light guys, and other assistants. They filmed for hours, came in production vans, had catering, and none of our segment even made it to television. The second thing to ponder was how smart television producers were in using free talent. Whether it was *American Idol* or *Battle for Ozzfest*, reality television worked because it was a cash cow for the networks. Everyone has a dream, especially in America. People would do crazy things for a one-in-a-million chance to become rich and famous. In this case, the kids were willing to travel the country on a tour bus and participate in all of this great footage for the benefit of MTV. I always hated this concept. Deep down, I thought it was kind of scummy how people's dreams were exploited.

It does remind me of a great story regarding my first love, Crystal. While we dated, like many other girls in their 20s, she wanted to be on *American Idol*. She was an amazing singer. She sang the national anthem at college basketball games and her voice was sultry and beautiful. The fact that she was stunningly beautiful didn't hurt, either. She figured at a minimum, it was good experience. For the two Eskimos out there who haven't seen *American Idol*, it follows the same formula every year. The judges visit a bunch of cities across the country where tens of thousands of hopefuls turn out for the chance to sing a verse, with the hopes of being discovered. This is all part of the marketing machine. The producers tap into every angle they can imagine. They play the "dream" and "being discovered" cards. They play the "chaos and excitement" card. They show the footage of people lined up for days and how they slept on the street just for their one chance at stardom. Quite frankly, it was obnoxious. America is so messed up when it comes to stuff like this. I didn't like the show because I feel it exploits all of these people. When Crystal wanted to do it, I tried to be the good boyfriend.

The casting came to Cleveland to hold tryouts at Cleveland Browns Stadium in the middle of the summer. The stadium holds over 70,000 people. Sure enough, all the local media played their role of making the *American Idol* arrival in town seem more important than the second coming of Christ. My sweet Crystal showed up about 5:00 a.m. and went into line with tens of thousands of other people. About 4:00 p.m., Crystal called me crying. Apparently, they were done with "casting" for the day, and they were going to keep everyone over night IN THE STADIUM. According to Crystal, thousands of people still in line were going to have to sleep overnight in the stadium unless they wanted to lose their spot and their slim chance at fame on day two. Crystal was given a seat location in the "Dawg Pound" – the end zone bleacher section of the stadium made famous by diehard Cleveland Browns fans (think beer bottle throwing and fights with Pittsburgh Steelers fans). Two shady looking guys were assigned to sit on each side of her. The participants were told they had to sleep in their seats and tryouts would start in the morning.

My friends know that Crystal was my little girl. She was a lot younger than I, and I always had this desire to protect her and take care of her. She would call me Superman and she was my little Lois Lane. When I called her phone, it would ring the "Superman Theme" she downloaded for me. I can still remember her crying, afraid that she would miss her dream and even more afraid that something creepy would happen to her overnight. Wasn't it absurd that in the name of television-excitement-crafting, some people thought this was acceptable? Yes, the stadium had bathrooms. Groups of people hung out together; some hung out on the ramps and in the tunnels of the venue. Apparently, however, participants were not allowed to bring in personal supplies. So, if someone wanted water, he had to pay $4 to buy it from the concession stand. It just rubbed me the wrong way, and they made my Crystal cry. I told her not to worry and that I would take care of it.

I needed a plan. One thing I knew was that *American Idol* was a Fox television show. I also knew that the other networks - ABC, NBC and CBS - likely hated *American Idol* because it was such a ratings giant. I called the local news desks of the other networks and told them my horrific tale. I acted a little dramatic. I warned of rapes and theft and anything else I could think of and painted the picture of how absurd and dangerous this scenario was and within 10 minutes, I had all three competing stations sending news vans to the scene. Immediately, reporters interviewed me over the phone, scheduled live shots, and most important, contacted the Cleveland Browns and *American Idol* producers seeking comment. It took about 30 minutes and the threat of the 6:00 p.m. news, but Crystal called me happy and informed me that everyone would be sent home with a secure place in line (numbered wristband) for the following day. Way to go, Superman! The day was saved once again.

This story reminds me what I tell people about political influence. Money is one way to get elected officials' attention. The other way to garner their attention is to go public with the story. No one wants to be the lead story on the news and in this case, *American Idol* had such great good will, this was the last thing they needed – competing television stations doing a story about the dangers of the tryouts.

I was thinking that *American Idol* has hundreds of thousands of people try out for the show and the contestants spend days just sitting around doing nothing while they are waiting. What a tremendous waste of human capital. I have done a lot of volunteer work. Could you imagine what tens of thousands of people mobilized for days could do to improve the community? Perhaps *American Idol* can save itself tons of production costs and having to listen to all of these awful singers by having would-be contestants complete a certain amount of community or volunteer service in order to participate in the tryouts. Maybe only 5,000 people would participate instead of 50,000, but imagine what 5,000 people could accomplish if they each did 10 hours of service in order to qualify! Something good could come out of a different approach. I had the same idea for jury duty. I had to sit in a waiting room for a whole week with hundreds of other people waiting to see if my jury service would be needed. I suggested that in the future, they give good citizens the chance to do some volunteer work while waiting. I love looking at a dumb or wasteful operation to try to figure out a way to improve it. Perhaps volunteers at jury duty could have edited this book and saved my eyes.

My Favorite Bitch, Omarosa

It is truly crazy how some people enter each other's lives. I mentioned my charity effort for Channel 3. One event I participated in led to one of my most interesting friendships – a friendship that continues to this day. I would classify myself as a "dear" friend of the one and only, Omarosa Manigault-Stallworth. Yep, that mean bitch from Donald Trump's *The Apprentice*.

Before I tease her too much, Omarosa is trustworthy, funny, generous, and sincere in her endless charity work. She just returned to a university in Dayton to pursue a faith ministry degree. Her story is an amazing one. She grew up poor in Youngstown, Ohio, and faced a lot of tough issues. It was dealing with those issues that shaped her and made her one of the strongest people I know. We always joke that if Omarosa and I were on an island with 50 serial killers, mark my words, the two of us would be the final two people alive on the island. I don't know how we would survive. I don't know what we would do. I just know that she and I "play for keeps," and if we had each other's resourcefulness to rely on, somehow we would emerge.

Before *The Apprentice*, Omarosa had a very successful life. She won scholarships, pageants, made a ton of money in real estate, worked in President Bill Clinton's White House and did a lot of other great things that made the producers of *The Apprentice* pick her out of hundreds of thousands of applicants. As the story goes, her answers on the producers' questionnaires were so raw and honest they knew they had a star. When posed with a question about how one would react to someone double-crossing him, every applicant gave some fluff answer about trying to talk about the situation, or work it out, or try for compromise, or some other bull that he didn't mean. What did Omarosa say? I'm making up the quote, but the message was basically, "If someone 'f's' with me, I don't know karate, but I know ca-razy (James Brown) and I will 'f' him with everything I have. "

The world's greatest "odd couple" – reality television star Omarosa and Mayor David Bentkowski.

Once on *The Apprentice*, it was clear to Omarosa that the best way to get air time and stay in the game was to be larger than life, controversial, and a force capable of taking out anyone in her way. I never watched the first season that she was on until after we were friends. Yes, if I had watched her actions originally, I would have hated her, too, just like the rest of America. The fact was, she was smart enough to know she was a character. She was and is the greatest villain in reality television history. In 50 years there will be books that talk about this weird reality television era, and she will remain as the most memorable character ever. Think about it, what realty television "stars" do people know? Maybe Richard Hatch from *Survivor*. Maybe Jen "what's her name" from *The Bachelorette*. Out of thousands that have been on the various shows, the most known is Omarosa.

There are so many interesting things to consider about Omarosa. When I met her, I had so many questions. What kind of cash did she secure from playing this villain? Did she know she was going to turn her 15 minutes of fame into years and years of being in the spotlight? What was her daily life like? Was it worth being the bad guy to have this awful image in exchange for the cash and celebrity? Just how hurtful was it to be demonized? Did she take it personally or did she just laugh at the notion that people were so consumed with celebrities? Did it bother her that even if people didn't know her, they spent so much time blogging about her? To this day, I love picking her brain about this stuff. Before I stray too far, let's talk about how we came to know each other.

I attended the "Gary Baxter Celebrity Bowl-A-Thon" to fight childhood obesity. Gary Baxter was an athletic defensive back when he played for the Baltimore Ravens. After he signed with the Cleveland Browns, he ruptured both of his Achilles tendons on the same play during a game. During one play his career was ruined. It is difficult to come back from one ruptured Achilles, and no one had ever come back from two. A good nickname for someone like Gary was "Hollywood." He was the star athlete; had the famous girl-friend (Michelle Williams of Destiny's Child); wore diamond earrings that would make Queen Elizabeth happy; and had that million-megawatt smile and personality that made people like him. Although I am sure there was a marketing and image component to it, I learned that Gary was close to his mother and friends and genuinely seemed to want to help a good cause. At his event, he had an auction of items that he collected from his teammates and celebrities. Rather than just go through the motions, Gary served as the auctioneer and pressured his rich celebrity friends to dig deeper and cough up more cash than they wanted to give. His charity effort was sincere.

At the event, I met Omarosa. She was a friend of Gary and Michelle's. The event was a blast. For 50 bucks to the charity, I bowled three games with the dozens of celebrities that showed up to help. I met Michelle Williams, Mario, Scott Williams, C.C. Sabathia, and a host of other Cleveland Browns and Cleveland Indians players. There was food, drinks, and the auction. What was cool about it was that I was assigned a lane and there was a celebrity assigned to bowl with me. However, while bowling, everyone was welcome to go from lane to lane and I met whomever I wanted. Since it was for charity and everyone was a friend of Gary's, the celebrities were unusually friendly and welcoming. There was a line of women waiting to meet Grady Sizemore of the Cleveland Indians. Smart guys were having bats and footballs signed by the athletes to later sell them on eBay for hundreds of dollars. I even challenged Michelle Williams to a one-frame winner-take-all contest – she rolled a strike using a pink eight-pound bowling ball and beat me. I had to turn in my Pollack card.

I met Omarosa because, well, she was being Omarosa. While all of the celebrities mostly stayed on their lane, Omarosa went from lane to lane and gave everyone some time. Her time with Bill Clinton paid off in her training. She was working the room like she was running for President. Celebri-

Mayor David Bentkowski and Michelle Williams of Destiny's Child at Gary Baxter's Celebrity Bowl-a-Thon.

Singer Mario and Mayor David Bentkowski.

Mayor David Bentkowski and Cy Young winner, pitcher C.C. Sabathia of the New York Yankees.

Mayor David Bentkowski with Outfielder Grady Sizemore of the Cleveland Indians.

ties are all about networking and making contacts. Lane by lane, Omarosa was making friends. It was interesting because love her or hate her, people want to meet her and talk to her so she was one of the big attractions of the night. It was just like watching her on television – or just like listening to Howard Stern – love them or hate them people want to see what they will do next. She could have just sat and bowled her games. Instead, she was making things happen. If another celebrity had an upcoming charity event, she learned about it and volunteered. If a celebrity was coming to Los Angeles, she was getting his info and offering to take him to dinner when he was in town. It was a great lesson. If she could help someone with nominal effort, then why wouldn't she? If she could grow a relationship with someone or gain a potentially beneficial contact, then why wouldn't she? Omarosa told me a story about Bill Clinton. When he would attend an event, by the time he was gone, he would have the entire room in love with him. The "magic" of Bill Clinton was that he made every person he met feel like they were the most important person in the world to him. I can envision Clinton meeting a fat middle-aged man and making a self-deprecating joke about his own weight so he could relate to that guy. I can envision Clinton meeting a woman and telling her some story about how she reminds him of his love, Hillary. I can envision Clinton meeting a chubby intern . . . well, that joke is too easy. Clinton had that gift of relating to people. When he held a woman's hand and looked into her eyes, she said to herself, "Wow, he's genuine or he cares about me." Of course, it is probably political poppycock – at least the slick part – but at the same time, politicians get a bad rap and Bill Clinton probably loved being that "character" and meeting different people, hearing their stories, and making them feel good. Why wouldn't he . . . it feels good to make other people feel special or good. Omarosa has that same gift. She would walk up to a young black woman and say, "Girl, that sweater is beautiful. I'm going to have to borrow that from you." Bet the house; that girl is going to school tomorrow and she is going to tell everyone she knows, "Omarosa loved my sweater." Again, these people are so good that it almost isn't calculated anymore. It may have been bull when they started out, but once they made it, they just enjoy making other people feel good.

Eventually Omarosa worked her way to my lane; Chris Matthews was with me to film video for my Channel 3 segments. Omarosa saw the camera and was a great sport. We did some shtick where she tried to trip me as I was bowling, and basically we both hammed it up and made some fun television footage. As we were talking, I asked her if she wanted to come on *Good Company* in the morning. I called producer Andrea Vecchio and she said they would love to have her. Omarosa came on the next morning. These were scenarios where everyone won. I won by getting a great guest for the show. She won by coming on the show and getting publicity. Of course, when she was on the show, she pretty much took over. In vintage Omarosa fashion, she was on for multiple segments. She was interviewed for her segment. Unscripted, she walked on camera during the cooking segment and said she was hungry and wanted to try the food. During the comedian segment, she came back on the couch and played a great supporting role. Incidentally, the comedian that day was Greg Fitzsimmons, and I will talk about him later. After the show, one of the most surreal lunches in the history of lunches took place. We were ready to leave the show about 11:30 a.m., so I said, "Hey, let's all go to lunch." Picture this table . . . Mayor David Bentkowski . . . Omarosa . . . Emmy-winning comedian Greg Fitzsimmons (probably the funniest comedian in the world), Michael Cardamone, John Lorince (the guy in charge of the comedians at Pickwick and Frolic/Hilarities, one of the nation's premier comedy clubs) and Chris Matthews. If we had a videotape of that lunch, we could sell it for 100 bucks. I don't know what was in the water that day, but it was non-stop jokes and every subject was fair game. At one point, Omarosa had something on her cheek and Michael was trying to wipe it off. I said, "Michael, she's black, that doesn't come off." I took great pleasure in making Greg Fitzsimmons laugh a bunch of times because just sitting there and listening to his jokes was a once-in-a-lifetime chance. The guy is off the charts hilarious.

After lunch I offered to take Omarosa back to her hotel. She stayed the extra day to do the show without checking to see if she could get her hotel room again. We got back to the hotel, and they told her she had to leave because they were booked. In fact, all of Cleveland was booked up with some convention. She had pushed back her flight until the next day, and she had nowhere to stay. Yep, the only option was to sleep at my house. Imagine that phone call to my mother and friends: "Hey, guess who's in my house? Yep, Omarosa from *The Apprentice.*" For those with dirty minds, I'll sat-

From left to right, Mayor David Bent-kowski, comedian Greg Fitzsimmons, Michael Cardamone and Omarosa on Good Company.

isfy your perverse curiosity and declare that there is no chance that Omarosa and I would ever be intimate. She dates famous people, athletes, models, and big black guys twice my size. I look at her like she's my sister. Besides, for a little white kid from the suburbs, I would be afraid to sleep with her. What if I did something wrong? She would probably yell at me and have me in tears. If I wanted that kind of danger and excitement, I'd go cliff-diving.

That night we hung out, went to dinner, and planted the seeds for a great friendship. I took her to the airport and wished her well. We kept in touch and sent each other funny texts. Some people knock texting, but I love it as a way to stay in touch with people. I have thousands of names and friends in my contact lists, so every now and then I like to send a text to hundreds of people. It might be a joke or it might be a quick holiday greeting. Mass text messages are also a great way to invite people to meet with me. I learned this from my friend Jen Simich, who is Mrs. Jen Verner after marrying Eddie. I used to tease Jen that she was like Puff Daddy or Sean John or P-Diddy or Sean Combs or whatever his name is now. P-Diddy is famous for being the life of the party. Jen was very good at sending out a text message letting everyone know where she was going that night. For example, I might get a text from her that said, "Eddie and I are going to the Indians game, and we are going to the Winking Lizard beforehand. Meet us up if you are out." Time after time I would get a text from her, and sure enough, I would be out and about and we could bump into each other. Maybe I was going to the game that night as well; and if I happened to be downtown before the game, then why wouldn't I want to bump into some friends? By sending out mass texts, Jen would simply create the opportunity for her friends to know where she was and create the opportunity to interact. Making plans with friends can be a chore. Maybe they live far away, maybe they have busy work schedules, or maybe I'm just not aware of their various interests. Receiving a text from a friend like Jen is great because it helps me stay in touch; I might be going to the same event five or six times a year and that's five or six times more that we can meet, and best of all, it helps me learn what that person likes to do. For example, if I go to five P-Funk concerts every year, sooner or later all of my friends I text are going to realize that they are my favorite group; as a result, maybe they buy me a P-Funk CD for Christmas or tell me they want to go with me to a future concert. It is just a great way to stay in touch and develop friendships. I call it the Puff Daddy factor because every time I would see Jen and Eddie out, they would have friends with them having great times – friends that probably responded to one of their texts. Likewise, that is what happened with Omarosa and me. We would check in with each other and remain interested in each other's events.

Omarosa was originally from Youngstown, about 40 minutes east of Cleveland, so whenever she came to town, we would hang out. We went to Browns games together, helped former Browns running back Rueben Droughns with his charity tailgate party, did the Baxter bowling event a second year, went to the Browns training camp in Berea (you should have seen all those young Browns players trying to get Omarosa's phone number) and went to dinners. We were the classic odd couple, always making each other laugh and always having each other's back.

Omarosa is friends with the LeVert family, the famous Cleveland soul singers. She came to town for Gerald LeVert's funeral. Omarosa came back again for the second LeVert tragedy, the death of Sean LeVert. As sad as those events were, there was a lighthearted moment that I will always remember. Omarosa was late flying into town and the location of the funeral home could have been hard to find if one weren't from Cleveland – it was in a pretty sketchy part of town. As always, I was happy to give my friend a ride when she needed one. She called me up and said, "Hey, can you drive me to LeVert's funeral wake?" I picked her up and drove her to the funeral home. It was a funny visual. I pull up with Omarosa and I was the only white dude around. Let's be honest, I am the whitest of white dudes. I look like every frat boy baseball player from the Midwest. A funeral in the black community is so different from what I am used to, especially the "calling hours" part. The family wanted the event to be private, but word of the location got out and people were just showing up at the funeral home. The inside was packed, and to help with crowd control, they had some guard – I don't know if he was with the funeral home or the city or where they got him – but this rent-a-cop was standing at the doors doing some ridiculous screening of who got in and who did not. There was no list or way to verify who was who, so one by one people were coming up to the door making their case as to why they should be allowed entry. I could have gotten in with Omarosa but that would have been ridiculous. Could you imagine a packed room of family and friends – crying, sobbing black folk – and then my "cracker" white butt? Needless to say, I wasn't about to distract these people in their moment of grief so I waited in the hallway by the door with the cop. This scene of people making their case to the cop was just so bizarre. I'm not exaggerating it, and I am not doing a stereotypical joke, but the dialogue was along the lines of "I'm friends with Marcus, Jamal's cousin, go ask so-and-so and they'll tell you the family would want me inside." Huh? Seriously, people were lobbying to be inside the funeral home. As mentioned, Officer Friendly had no formula or methodology as to who got in and who didn't. I watched it for a half-hour and will tell you access was pretty much based on who was cool and convincing versus those who got to the door and panicked at the question of "Who are you?" Word eventually got out that the cop was only letting in family, so eventually everyone who would come up to the door claimed they were a cousin or in-law or brother. I even saw a couple of people that were initially denied come back without their coats or with a different shirt on and proudly state that yes, they were family, and they gained entry. I'm pretty sure that ultimately everyone gained access at one point or another. I only tell this story because it was so interesting to see the cultural difference between a black funeral wake and a white funeral wake.

Aside from that door fiasco, something else memorable happened. After she was inside for a half-hour, Omarosa came outside, stood on the steps, and said hello to people. There was a famous singer who showed up whom I think was from The O'Jays. As this guy walked up the steps, he was decked out like a pimp. I don't mean that in a bad way because some guys can look fairly stylish in those types of outfits – you know what I'm talking about – a giant pin-striped suit, double-breasted, huge scarf, funky hat, white shoes, loud jewelry, etc. The dude walked up with a beautiful woman who was dressed sharply, but flashily. Okay, I won't sugarcoat it too much. She looked like she was just in a Snoop Dog rap video. It was not that she was dressed inappropriately, but the Good Lord had just blessed her with certain curves and badda-bing features that made her stand out from everyone else. In a deadly serious voice, this famous singer said, "Omarosa, I want you to meet my lady friend." I swear I almost choked on my gum. I'm thinking to myself, "Did he just say that – really – he can get away with introducing someone like that?" As soon as he said it, in the sweetest, softest black-woman voice, the "lady" said, "Hiiiiiiiii" – kind of long and drawn out the way a black girl might say, "Heeeeyyyyyyy." That, my friends, is when you are the man - when you can dead-seriously introduce a woman as your "lady friend."

Omarosa said, "You got a name, lady friend?" That would be the day when a boyfriend tries to call Omarosa that. I'm sorry that something funny happened at such a sad event and my prayers go out to the LeVert family, but to this day my friends and I try to sneak in a "lady friend" reference whenever we can. I drove Omarosa nuts the next couple times she was in town because I kept introducing her as my "lady friend" with my best Barry White voice. It was all in good fun, but it was interesting to be exposed to the black community's culture. Could you imagine if I introduced a girlfriend at some city function as my "lady friend" – she would have been like, "Are you serious?" and would have punched me in my face. I guess I'm not quite yet a pimp or player that could pull it off smoothly.

I mentioned how this "lady friend" introduction struck me as being a funny cultural difference moment and it reminded me of similar scenarios. As I've said, Omarosa is a sincere, accommodating person in real life, and I have seen it with my own eyes. I was impressed by the way people react to her. Keep in mind she was famous for being the "bitch" or the "villain" – the over-the-top personality. So it was very interesting to see what people said to her when they met her. I have seen dozens of younger white guys like me come up to her and say, "Oh my God, Omarosa, you were awesome. You were such a bitch! Will you take a picture with me? I can't wait to tell everyone I met you." She was always a good sport. She went out of her way to give them the picture they wanted. She would pose and pretend to choke the guy in the picture or pretend to punch him. I couldn't walk up to any other woman and say, "Oh my God, you're such a bitch! I would love to have a picture with you." Her being a bitch was just a character, and she would play along with it for their benefit. A frat guy who has a picture with Omarosa choking him was going to impress his buddies with the story of his meeting.

Omarosa was insightful when she talked about this role-playing. She recently wrote a book called *The Bitch Switch* for Phoenix Books, and she discussed attitude and people's perceptions. For example, if a guy was aggressive and demanding and knew what he wanted, he was viewed as powerful and smart, like a Donald Trump. If a woman spoke her mind and played tough, she was a bitch. *The Apprentice* was a contest – winner take all - so wasn't it interesting that Omarosa was viewed as a huge bitch for the way she played the game? In a football game, the team players try to rip each other's heads off, tackle, use deception on every play and use every other trick in the book for an edge. Why was *The Apprentice* contest any different? She wanted to win, and she played a character and did things to win.

One thing I learned about Omarosa was that she was generous and loyal to those around her. She was always helping out her mom, her nephews, her friends and anyone else she could. In my case, she opened up several great adventures including my participation on *The Celebrity Apprentice*. That crazy week I spent in New York involved many celebrities and subplots, so I am going to give it its own chapter, but make no mistake about it, Omarosa made it happen.

The Celebrity Apprentice: "David, how fast can you get to New York?"

On a Thursday night in October about 10:00 p.m., I had just taken my dogs Grace and Liberty out and was getting ready for bed. The phone rang and on the other end was a very weary-sounding Omarosa. She had been filming *The Celebrity Apprentice* in New York in 2007. *The Apprentice*, the show where young upstarts compete to work for Donald Trump, had lost a little thunder over the years, and so in an effort to breathe some new life into the formula, there was an idea to do *The Celebrity Apprentice* where a diverse group of celebrities would participate and earn money for charity. The first *Celebrity Apprentice* had the likes of Heavyweight Boxing Champion of the World, Lennox Lewis; Vincent Pastore of *The Sopranos*; Olympic champions like softball's Jenny Finch and the legendary gymnast Nadia Comaneci; actor Stephen Baldwin; Supermodel Carol Alt; and, of course, Omarosa. When she was first cast on the show, I remember reading a bunch of people online saying, "Omarosa? She's not a celebrity." Those people didn't know television. Omarosa was probably the biggest reason people watched that show. Love her or hate her, people were tuning in to see what she would do next. Don't let anyone fool you - these television people knew what they were doing and the odds of becoming famous or landing a show are very small. Omarosa wouldn't still be around if she didn't have a big impact on viewership. Think of how many people were on hit shows that couldn't get a bit part anymore. Fame is fleeting and the people behind *Celebrity Apprentice* wisely used Omarosa to generate interest. I remember during the show's initial advertising and marketing that they would name some of the celebrity candidates and then end with Omarosa – in a sort of "the bitch is back" or *Terminator* "I'm baaaack" kind of imagery. Absolutely, America wanted to see Omarosa tell another celebrity to "f" off – that's good television. Joan Rivers was great on the second *Celebrity Apprentice* for the same reason.

Omarosa had filmed about four or five episodes already when she called me. If you have never seen the show, the players are on teams, and they are given a business assignment by Donald Trump at the start of the day. The tasks or challenges can be wide ranging, but they have something to do with business. The teams then work on the task all day and night, and the following morning, until they are summoned into the board room to face "The Donald" and his scrutiny. If "The Donald" felt a player caused his team to lose, he barked those classic words, "You're fired!" The board room scenes are memorable battles where each player pleads his case to Trump in an effort to save his own life. When sitting in a board room with Omarosa, look out, because she will use everything she has. Trump can be swayed and viewers at home love to guess whom he will fire. It is a good concept and show, and there are a lot of business lessons to be learned – and who better to learn them from than one of America's greatest entrepreneurs, Donald Trump.

Always one to challenge the rules and look for any possible edge, Omarosa called me up and said, "I think I might be able to use you to help me on the show. The rules (yes, they have a giant packet of materials that guide what the players can and can't do) stated that the players could use helpers on various tasks. When they said helpers, they meant carpenters or electricians or other professional people. On the show, a lot of the tasks are complex. One of the episodes I helped on was a tie-in with Vera Wang and Serta Mattress. The pair was doing a home line together and the task was to create a storefront window that did justice to Vera Wang's amazing style and the quality and comfort of a Serta Mattress. As you could imagine, creating this New York storefront window space in one day involved electricians hanging up lighting, carpenters creating sets and displays, and a bunch of other technical stuff that couldn't be done by the celebrities. Even though the celebrities do a vast majority of the work, let's be real, Lennox Lewis isn't wiring spotlights. Omarosa felt that the rules didn't stipulate who could be hired as a helper or not. She thought it would be incredibly helpful to her team – and her especially – to have a "friend" helping in New York whom she could trust. New York is one of my favorite places in the world. I fell in love with it that first crazy trip when I was on Howard Stern and have been back over 100 times.

I absolutely love the city and know it like the back of my hand. Omarosa called me on Thursday and said, "Our next task is tomorrow morning at 8:00 a.m.; can you be here and help me?" What do I do when I have a once-in-a-lifetime chance for adventure . . . or a great story . . . or a chance at fame and fortune . . . or even just the chance to break up the routine of life? You bet your ass – I take it!

I called my trusty wing-man Chris Matthews and asked him if he wanted to go. Of course he did – there is a reason he is my wing-man. Within a half-hour, we were out the door and driving seven hours through the night toward the Big Apple. I accept that most sane people would never do this. Most people would pause and think better of it. They would think of every excuse not to go. Maybe they had a job. Maybe they have kids. There were no guarantees that anything would come of this. I could have shown up in New York and the producers could have said, "Sorry, you can't participate." It could have been a waste of 14 hours of driving for the round-trip for absolutely nothing. Or, it could be an incredible chance to be behind the scenes of a network television show. In life, you are either the type of person who is going to roll the dice and put himself in a position for something great to happen, or, you are going to be the person who spends his life wondering what could have happened if he had tried various things. Life is short and I am going to get my money's worth. Wondering "what could have happened" is not something that I will ever have to do. Good or bad, I will have an answer because I will try it.

We drove through the night and got to the George Washington Bridge. There was a broken-down truck on the bridge and it took about an hour just to get over the bridge. The whole time we were stuck in traffic, Omarosa is frantically texting me to get there because they were going to let her use me. I finally showed up, and, trust me; I got caught up in the excitement of the contest. Omarosa kept talking in "code" because all of the phone calls are taped for possible use on the show. The phones they use are supplied by the show. I felt like I was some secret agent trying to piece together what my role was. I was totally exhausted near the end of the drive, but the minute I set foot on Manhattan, "it was on, like Donkey Kong!" We picked up Omarosa's mother Theresa, better known as Momarosa, from the hotel. Chris and Momarosa dropped me off at the office where they were filming and their instructions were "keep driving around New York with the car in case you are needed." I rushed upstairs, signed a bunch of release forms that there was no time to read, and was wired for sound. Right away, I sensed this was a big-time, network television production. There were cameras and workers and crews all over the place. Finally, I was ready to go. The conference room doors opened up, and with a film crew in my face, Omarosa ran to greet me. The first few weeks of *Celebrity Apprentice*, the teams were split up with the men on one side and the women on the other. The "girls" team kept losing and Omarosa thought it would be a good storyline if I showed up and helped her. The concept was one that probably would have played well had it been used, and judging by how much they filmed me, my guess is they probably were at least thinking about it. Omarosa called her young mayor friend in Cleveland at 10:00 p.m., he drove through the night to go help her, he showed up on zero sleep, busted his tail for her team all day, the girls finally won a task with his assistance, and the mayor saved the day and helped his friend. It would have been good. Truth is an even better storyline emerged when Vincent Pastore of *The Sopranos* was involved in a plot that sort of mirrored something that would happen on that famous mafia show. I don't remember all the details but he left the men's team, then he came to the women's team, but then they caught him giving secrets about the women to the men's team; Omarosa found out, chaos ensued, drama, drama, drama – so there was no big television break for David Bentkowski.

The "creative" thing Omarosa did was hire me for whatever the task was. On my first day, the team needed pictures of New York taken for some ad campaign assignment so Omarosa said I was her professional photographer. On day two, there were items that the team finished building at a warehouse, so she said I was a professional mover, and I made time-saving deliveries. It was hilarious to see her explaining this to the producers. They obviously figured out the gig by day two, and I think they were amused by her antics. Picture someone from the show saying to her, "Wait a minute, yesterday he was your photographer and today he is the moving guy?" Picture Omarosa saying, "That's right, and tomorrow he is going to be my painter and paint the store window for Vera Wang." Whatever the task was, assuming it wasn't some professional task like wiring, she was going to assign it to me because she knew she could trust me, knew that I knew New York, and knew that I

Mayor David Bentkowski with super-model Carol Alt and actor Stephen Baldwin on the set of The Celebrity Apprentice.

would genuinely do all I could to help her team versus some guy she would hire out of the phone book who didn't care if she won or not. The thing about *The Apprentice* is that if your team wins the task, no one on your team gets "fired" by Trump. So even though everyone was like "who the heck is that" when I first walked in, I soon became a resource for everyone on her team, which included Mari Lou Henner from *Taxi* fame, super-model Carol Alt, Nely Galon (the creator of *The Swan* and Telemundo fame), and eventually actor Stephen Baldwin.

Picture the scene that first day: I hadn't slept for nearly two days. I had just driven from Cleveland to New York, everything was happening at whirlwind speed, and by 11:00 a.m., I had a film crew in my face as I worked on an ad campaign with Carol Alt, who is still gorgeous. Meanwhile, Chris and Momarosa were still driving around New York waiting for instructions I couldn't give them because I was wearing a recorded microphone and not allowed to call anyone.

Although I did work hard and helped the "girls'" team, the fact is the producers would never let me interfere with the outcome of the episode, and the girls won on their own merit. My assistance basically served as a chance for the team to handle a grueling work schedule. One thing I was truly amazed at is how hard they work these celebrities. They wake up and are in hair and makeup around 6:00 a.m. By 8:00 a.m., they are getting their task from Trump. They spend the entire day, non-stop, working until 1:00 a.m. They start the day at 6:00 a.m. again the following morning and finish their task until they are taken to the Trump board room that afternoon. I am not kidding, celebrities or not, they bust their butts and are worked like I couldn't believe.

I was in New York helping on the show for about five or six days. Oh, the stories I could tell about what happened behind the scenes. The whole thing was cool. I learned so much about television, business, celebrity, New York, and many other things from being thrust into this scenario. Imagine driving around New York and parking a car anywhere you wanted because you had a special "film" permit from Mayor Mike Bloomberg's office. Imagine making a food run for supermodel Carol Alt, and bringing her back two magazines where she is on the cover, which you saw while standing in line at Whole Foods. Imagine at the end of the day being driven back to Trump Tower in a van with a film crew and Omarosa, Stephen Baldwin, Mari Lou Henner, Nely Galon and Carol Alt. Crazy stuff always happens to me when I go to New York.

Eventually, the gig was up and the producers had enough of my existence. They were probably wise to shut me down because if I had kept on my current pace, there probably would have been an episode where Trump called me into the board room and said, "Kid, who are you and why did you sabotage Lennox Lewis?" The interesting thing about television is that I was filmed for days. I was in every key scene, and I was right there in the trenches with all of the celebrities. Yet, when the episodes finally aired, viewers could see about 10 glimpses of me in the background totaling about 15 seconds. As usual, my big moment turned out to be a dud and opened the door for family and friends to tease me. Whenever I was working on a task, I would be running all over New York trying to get things done. When I came back to the "base" where the celebrities were working, it would be the only time during the day when I had a few moments to sit down, catch my breath, and grab something to eat. Every time I was on television, I was shoving a doughnut or sandwich down my throat because I would only have a few minutes until I was off again. When the show aired on NBC, I would get text after text saying, "Dude, what the heck, every time you are on, you are eating in the background?" It sucked I wasn't on more, but at least I was on enough for everyone to see me and, of course, tease me about eating.

I shared this story about *The Celebrity Apprentice* because if it weren't for Omarosa and her interest in including me, her friend, it would have never happened. I hate to sound like "Clarence the Angel," but just like we learned in *It's a Wonderful Life*, it is amazing how life can be impacted by one event or person. If I never had met Bill Safos, I would never have done my charity show on Channel 3. If I never had met Tom Goebel, my show sponsor, ditto. If I never did my charity show, and if I never went to the Gary Baxter Bowl-A-Thon, I never would have met Omarosa. If I didn't ask Omarosa to go on *Good Company* the following day, we never would have kept in contact. If I didn't invite her to stay at my house or offer to take her to the airport, we never would have bonded as friends. If we never bonded as friends, we wouldn't have stayed in touch and had all those great stories. If we didn't stay in touch, I never would have been on *Celebrity Apprentice* nor had the chance to participate the way I did. After *Celebrity Apprentice*, Omarosa was roasted in New York by the Friars Club. I went to support her and a whole bunch of other crazy stories happened during that trip. The Friars aren't exactly "spring chickens" and there was a slate of hilarious comedians roasting Omarosa and the crowd. I was sitting next to some lady that had to be 120 years old, and she was wearing an ugly, multi-colored sweater. Funny comedian Rich Voss was picking on everyone in the crowd and he looked at her and said, "Lady, your sweater is the ugliest sweater I have ever seen. It looks like a box of crayons jerked off on you." I did a spit-take and spilled my drink.

Just this year, Omarosa took me to the Book Expo of America in New York City. She won an award for her book and invited me to tag along. Thanks to her, I met Matthew Donnelley and Katie Steigman of Greenleaf Book Group. These two "kids" played a crucial role in launching this book, and I am forever grateful. They said my idea was a good one, and they told me how to make it happen. Isn't that such a typical story for me? Out of hundreds of exhibitors, I walked up to these two kids and just started talking to them about my book, and they helped me make it happen. People spend years trying to figure this stuff out, and I was graced to walk right up to these two and be on my way.

While at the book expo, Wesley Snipes was there because he also won an award. My camera was acting funny and the picture Wesley posed for with me didn't come out very well. So, there are about 10 pictures of me standing behind Wesley while he is sitting at a table, and Omarosa was snapping away

Mayor David Bentkowski with rap pioneer Dana Dane at the Book Expo of America in New York.

Mayor David Bentkowski with actor Wesley Snipes at the Book Expo of America in New York.

for me trying to get one that I could use. Finally he looked at me like, "Crazy white boy, what are you doing behind me?" For you hard core hip-hop fans, I also hung out with Dana Dane and also met sportscaster James Brown and author Joe Scarborough.

The point is I never know how things will unfold or how people will come and go in my life. Omarosa and I are truly the ultimate odd couple. The realty television star who is famous for being a bitch is great friends with the small town mayor who is considered laid-back and easygoing. Yet, somehow it works. Life is about meeting interesting people and having interesting adventures. I don't know what crazy thing will happen next to me or Omarosa, but I am sure it will be something.

Martha Stewart: Polish Perfection

As I am writing this, I have officially hit rock bottom. I am sitting on an Amtrak train heading from New York back to cold Cleveland. Don't get me wrong, I normally love riding the Amtrak. I purposely started taking it in order to write this book. I love to go to New York and have a ton of friends in the city. I have made the drive or flown many times, and I was thrilled when I discovered the train option because it is just better. If I were going to fly to New York from Cleveland, it's at least $150 each way even with advance booking, which I never seem to do. The cab ride from *JFK* or Newark to Manhattan is around $50. Add in all the extras, and flying is expensive. I have made the drive many times and it is no bargain either. For starters, I am arguably the worst driver in history. Every time I drive through the hills of Pennsylvania on my way to New York, it is amazing I don't kill myself or others. It always seems like it is foggy; there are crazy turns throughout the mountains and hills; there are angry semi-drivers; and after about seven hours, my neck feels like someone is stabbing it and I am so stressed. Plus, the cost stinks as well. It takes tanks of gasoline, $18 just to cross the George Washington Bridge to get into New York, and $35 a day to park in the city.

The train, on the other hand, is the deal of the century. For $60 each way, it picks me up by Cleveland Browns Stadium in downtown Cleveland (yes, at 3:00 a.m., which sucks, but what am I going to do?) Once on the train, it is about a 12-hour ride through scenic America and it stops at Penn Station right in Madison Square Garden on 33rd and 8th Avenue in downtown Manhattan. From there, it costs me $1.50 to take a subway to any number of friends' locations. Not only is it the cheapest option, it is safe; I don't have to drive or fly, there is no rigorous security to go through, the seats are wide and comfortable, and best of all, I could sit in the café car to write this book. The café car was filled with booths like one I would sit in at a Denny's. There were power outlets for my laptop. The train also served alcohol. I keep telling my friends we should do a group outing. Imagine 12 hours on the train with your best friends drinking and playing cards while enjoying the view on your way to New York. We could play RISK and Texas Hold 'em and share stories for hours and hours, something we do all the time anyway.

I mentioned that on this particular day I have hit rock bottom because, for whatever reason, the train I am on today does not have a café car. The train is sold out, and every seat is filled. I was sitting by myself when a ridiculously cute couple came up to me and asked if they could have my seat so they could sit together and asked if I could sit across the aisle next to some women that had an open seat. It was one of those classic, "I hate to bother you" moments. Well, if someone hates to bother me, then don't. I love those insincere qualifying statements because they are always followed by the very action they supposedly denounce.

I am not amused because the woman I am sitting next to made it publicly known to most of the train her disgust that I was going to occupy the seat next to her. She has turned her body at an angle away from me like she is in a tornado position and has been mumbling and grumbling for the last 10 minutes. Best of all, she has built a territorial fort like a five-year-old – a dividing wall of her stuff between us. She is obnoxiously eating food loudly and she smells like cabbage. I have sat here for about 10 minutes trying not to breathe or move, trying to help diffuse the situation. But, I've just decided, the heck with it – I am going to whip out the laptop and type away. I am about as aggressive as a butterfly so what does she want from me? Either it would be me sitting next to her or one of these other likely felons on the train: so pick your poison, lady.

Here is what is making me feel bad: the two lovebirds next to me. For starters, if they hug and kiss and snuggle and do any other cute thing again, I am going to punch both of them. I just hate when people are in love like that when I am not. They have a "Learn Greek" book and are practicing learning the language together. Every now and then there must be a Greek word for "kitten" or "cutie" or "snuggle puss" or some other pet name that causes them to call each other that word and then giggle and kiss. I want to vomit! I want to vomit because I am as sad as I have been with my relationship life for a long time. I am finally accepting that my last relationship is over; we are not going to be together. I can't even comprehend what divorce must feel like, and I wouldn't wish it on my worst enemy.

I am someone who is known as a serious dater. I have been with two girls in the last six years. I am at the point in my life where I am trying to find the person I am going to start a family with and spend the rest of my life with or I am going to "punt" and just live a wild, single life. I am not interested in casual dating that just wastes time. I am way beyond that. Every time I meet someone new, I approach the relationship with the intention of determining if she could be the "one." I am Polish and Croatian. My parents have been together for nearly 50 years, so in my mind I have a vision of what a relationship should be and mean.

What does this all have to do with Martha Stewart? Well, that's easy. When I think about relationships and always doing the right thing and always acting with a sense of compassion and decency – I think about being unselfish and making sacrifice for a greater love - I think of my mother, Barbara, the greatest woman in the world. My mother is the Martha Stewart of the Midwest, and the two have so much in common.

Of all the things that make me believe in God, the gift of my mother is one of the most compelling. Of course, I am biased, but the fact is this amazing woman has never failed anyone. She has the amazing qualities a lot of moms have and she gives love like no other. She created a special household for my siblings and me while we grew up. She would love and defend me even if I climbed a tower and gunned down a town. She is the one person who always has my back no matter what. She is the one person who never wants anything from me, and she dedicates her entire life to selflessly doing things for me. She is every positive adjective I can think of: loving, kind, generous, helpful, gracious, classy, sophisticated, thoughtful, beautiful, amazing, sincere and a million more words. But of all her great qualities, she is inspiring because she leads by example.

I do not have one of those weird complexes where I will never be able to find a good girlfriend or wife because I don't think she will "compare" with Mom. In fact, Mom has always been a firm believer that when a man finds his wife, the wife comes first and he puts her and his new family above everyone else, including Mom. Mom's greatest dream and desire is for me to find someone who makes me happy and to start a wonderful family with that woman.

Barbara Bentkowski in the 1970s.

Sometimes women don't grasp this or they feel intimidated by a strong mother/son relationship, but they are making a mistake because the greatest "card" she could play is to give Mom her "props" because she will become her greatest ally. Although I do want to find a great girl and get married, Mom's example is often a great barometer of whether or not a new girl is right for me.

She is out there and when I find her, it will be special, but it would be helpful for some girls reading this to learn and ponder Mom's story. This isn't a relationship book, but here are some great life lessons from the way Mom is compared to the way younger girls are today.

For starters, I hate the show *Sex in the City*. Various girlfriends have attempted to force me to catch an episode every now and then, and I would rather stab myself in the balls with a butter knife than ever watch it again. I don't mean to offend, but a lot of women have a delusion about what life owes them, and it is perpetuated by stupid shows like this. I cannot stand girls that refer to themselves as "princesses" or "divas." Really? They want people to think of them like that? Some girls think life is eating sushi, going to wine bars, and buying $400 jeans. That's not real life, that's television. I am all for equal rights and women establishing their own independence but as part of this women's "movement" many women have chosen to act what I would deem as "ugly" and have left behind the very beautiful, gracious qualities that make women so attractive to men in the first place.

I would love for my wife to make $500,000 a year. I wouldn't be jealous or insecure a bit. I would love for my wife to achieve a great career and be a powerful executive or whatever else she wanted to become in life. Her success would be amazing to me. Basically, I want my wife or girlfriend to

Mayor David Bentkowski with his mother, Barbara Bentkowski, at his second inauguration.

be my partner, my equal. I want her to be my best friend. I want us to be a team; two people who are in it together against the rest of the world. I want her to be the one person in the world I can always count on, the person I would make that forever promise to be by her side no matter what – just like the vows say – in good times and bad, in sickness and health and until death do us part. When a girl acts ugly and selfish, it is a turn-off; I question if she is going to be like that with our kids or if we hit a rough patch? This isn't about Mom, but her example helps make the point. Mom would never pay $75 to have her nails done. She would rather take that $75 and give it to the grandkids. Mom would never pay $400 for jeans - she would rather exercise and look beautiful for Dad even if she were in $5 jeans. Mom would never flirt with other guys or treat someone's feelings as disposable. Mom would bear as much pain as she could take so someone else didn't have to suffer. It's not the jeans or the nails or the partying attitude that makes Mom amazing. It's the fact that everything she does is out of love and with humility toward others.

I know so many wonderful moms. Theresa Shumay, Joe's mom, raised 10 kids. She and her husband Tom started with nothing and built a fulfilling life together. Their 10 kids have finished college, started families, run businesses, made thousands of friends, and produced dozens of grandkids. Theresa and Tom have a lifetime of happiness, love and memories that they created together with hard work and an unselfish take on life. Mrs. Shumay is a grand matron, and it is so heartwarming to see all the kids and grandkids shower her with love and gifts and respect because they know she has earned it and deserves it.

One of the hardest deaths of my life was the passing of Chris Matthews' mom, Andrea. I loved her so much and loved how she was always so positive. When Chris and I were in high school, Andrea was cleaning houses to make some extra money to help the family. She was cleaning some rich bitch's house, and Chris and I were with her after school. I just remember this obnoxious client being so dramatic about all she had to do, how the house was such a mess, blah, blah, blah. I can remember Andrea being kind and humble and assuring this lazy slob that she would help her and take care of it all. Like Cinderella, she swallowed her pride for the paycheck from this ugly soul who wasn't half the person she was. The day Andrea, my mom, Theresa Shumay, or many other great women I know would have a house cleaner and act proud and uppity to her would never happen. If I had millions and sent a house cleaner to my mother's house, my mother would join her or say she had to do it a certain way to make the cleaner stop because she wouldn't be comfortable with someone serving her like that. Andrea worked her tail cleaning that house; when she was done, she left with her head held high with dignity. She did what she had to do to make a better life for people she loved. Her actions were much more important than the vanity of the woman acting so overwhelmed with her spoiled life. It is okay to have help and a housecleaner, but it was the way the woman treated Andrea that was pathetic.

Pattie Maffo is Tim's mom, and a cancer survivor. She is another great mom that treats me like her own son. One of my favorite charities to support is the Susan G. Komen Foundation for breast cancer awareness. Breast cancer can take our moms, sisters, wives and girlfriends, so every guy should step up and help raise money to find a cure.

Speaking of someone special, I am not going to lie, I love Martha Stewart. By now, you can tell that Mom is just like Martha Stewart. My mother has every talent Martha has and the holidays she gave us would give Martha a run for her money. I say this in tribute to Martha because I believe she has amazing gifts, and I am thankful to her for sharing them with the world. Like Mom, Martha Stewart is Polish. Maybe it's a generational and ethnic thing, but people like Mom and Martha work hard. They learned from more difficult times. They paid their dues and have decades of experience. To this day, my mother and Martha Stewart, both in their 60s, work as hard as anyone I know. Now that they have earned their respect and place, they aren't about to slow down because they know what it took to achieve that success.

I was doing my charity segments for Channel 5 WEWS/ABC in Cleveland while they were launching Martha Stewart's new television show. Just like Gwen Stefani, Martha realized her visit had to match her image so she had her meet and greet at the Cleveland Botanical Garden. Phyllis Sossi, my friend from Channel 5 and another great mom, asked me if I could give Martha a proclamation celebrating her visit to Cleveland. I said, yes, because I wanted to meet Martha and tell her that I was Polish and that my mom was amazing just like her. Plus I figured there had to be a way to make meeting Martha beneficial for Seven Hills. Of all the people I have met, Martha Stewart is as commanding a presence as anyone. She didn't earn nearly a billion dollars in her life by being some shrinking violet. Martha entered the beautifully decorated Botanical Garden's grand hall to hundreds of adoring fans and show sponsors.

Don't ask me how or why, but somehow her "meeting the mayor" was given top billing. As soon as she walked into the room she was brought over to me for our introduction and proclamation exchange. Martha Stewart in person was absolutely beautiful. Her skin was flawless, she had a sexy "womanly" figure, and she had poise and grace. I mentioned her presence; the people in the room just froze watching her. It was like they were afraid to go up to her at first. It was so interesting to witness. Of course, I have no problem talking to anyone, so I jumped right into my gibberish and started making conversation with Martha Stewart. The reality is I am a guy who plays sports and scratches himself. I never watch "chick" movies, and quite frankly, I think the Lifetime Channel should be eliminated because in every movie, the guy is the bad guy and the wife ends up killing him. I didn't have a lot to talk about with Martha Stewart. I gave her the proclamation – I gave her some of my best lines like "I'm Polish as well and Mom cooks pierogies on Christmas Eve." Martha was sweet and kind and pretended to give a darn about what I had to say. The funny part is, after about 10 minutes, we were still standing there talking to each other one on one. Mind you, she was only going to be there for an hour and there were hundreds of people in the room who wanted to meet her. However, because everyone was awestruck, she spent the first 10 minutes talking to me. I kid you not, after 10 minutes

I didn't have anything else to talk about with her, so I left her. I was the one that said, "Okay, well, it was great meeting you. Maybe you should go say 'hi' to some of these other folks. Hope to see you again." I waved some new people over to us and that opened the flood gates. Martha was gracious and talked with everyone in the room. She took pictures, told great stories, and brought gifts for everyone in attendance. Everyone that came received a Martha Stewart Macy's spatula, cookbooks, duffle bags, and magazines.

After I was done talking with Martha, I spotted a beautiful girl standing in the corner on her phone. I couldn't leave yet, so I walked over to her and eventually struck up a conversation with her. Turns out, it was Martha's personal assistant Liesl Menning. Liesl was Martha's right-hand girl. There have been several times when Liesl would be in a New York newspaper photo walking with Martha – like one of those paparazzi shots where they are photographed coming out of a coffee shop or walking the dogs. On several occasions, the papers would mistakenly think Liesl was Martha's daughter, Alexis. As sweet as Martha was, talking to Liesl was much more interesting to me because of my public relations background. I figured Liesl would be the one with all the stories. What's it like working for Martha, what does the job entail, tell me some cool stories, etc. Liesl has a million-dollar personality, and we laughed and talked for the next 50 minutes. When I look back, we probably hit it off so much because after some initial Martha jokes and questions, I wanted to learn more about Liesl. It takes a very talented person in her own right to be the person behind the scenes who manages Martha's life and Liesl was incredibly interesting to me. We exchanged cell numbers and promised to keep in touch, and we did. Maybe it was because we had such a good first meeting or maybe it was because I had a mayor's title so I didn't strike her as some lunatic stalker or fan. She was always so professional. She would never reveal any of Martha's confidences, but she would share her funny personal stories which were often a result of her job. We talked about the night she was watching Martha's dogs in the Hamptons. We talked about her father who was a decorated pilot for our great country. We talked about her new boyfriend who she eventually married. When we talked, it was a sincere interest in one another's life.

Liesl is a great example of meeting good people by networking. I hate when people meet people to try and use them. People try to kiss my butt all

Mayor David Bentkowski gives a proc-lamation to domestic goddess, Martha Stewart at Cleveland Botanical Gardens.

the time, and they usually have some agenda. When I met Liesl, it led to a genuine friendship. I sent her honey wine from my friend Dave Jilbert's farm, Jhel-baire Winery, in Valley City, because she had never had it before, and I was excited that I might introduce her and Martha to something new. When I went to NYC, instead of expecting some star-studded entertaining, I had more fun when Liesl and I went to dinner with her little niece who was visiting. To this day, I am Facebook friends with her and her family and I am looking forward to visiting with her and her new husband.

This chapter helped me clarify in my mind what I want in life as far as happiness and a companion. The great women I have met in my life, whether Barbara Bentkowski or Martha Stewart, have given me countless lessons to apply to my relationships. Now that I have had my epiphany, my dating future is solely in my hands.

As I finish this chapter, the young couple in love is fighting because the guy spilled something on her apparently expensive outfit. Kids . . . I hope they can work it out.

Ladies Love Cool J and Cool Dave

My penis is exactly seven and three quarter inches long and almost three of my fingers wide. Ha-ha, I bet you didn't see that coming! I know this because like every other male in the world, at least the honest ones who will admit it, I have measured it many times in my life. So, what does this information have to do with LL Cool J? Well, of all the celebrities I have met, I am just speculating that in his youth, LL Cool J probably used his penis more than a lot of other people. I'll get to that in a second, but let me share with the ladies some thoughts and points about the male penis that they may not know.

There have been several studies done across the globe, and most of them reveal the same thing: around 90% of men have an erect penis between five and seven inches. So, although I certainly don't claim to be some porn star, I want to thank my parents for the great genes and for being able to "hold my own" – something I have done many times. Ladies, don't let our bluffing fool you; it's a guy thing to want to have a swagger or a bragging right about something. It's like a buck showing off his antlers. We want to show other guys that we are no slouches. I may not be a porn star, but in my mind, "Hey, I'm bigger than at least 90% of all guys so I'll take it." It's just that little accomplishment that makes a guy feel like he can compete with other guys. Maybe you are the guy who can bench press 300 pounds . . . maybe you are the fastest guy on your football team . . . maybe you have a bank account like Trump. Whatever . . . we all want to have as many honor badges as we can and "packing" is definitely a great one to have in the "check" column.

The second thing to know about the penis is that there are no "tells" about what a guy might have. It doesn't matter if a guy is tall or short . . . it doesn't matter the size of his feet, or his nose, or his hands . . . and according to studies, his race or ethnicity doesn't matter either. I have seen guys six-foot-five that have a stub, and I have seen a guy five-foot-five that had an "apparatus" that looked like a baby's arm holding an apple. I have seen these things because boys have no problem embarrassing their buddy in the shower. If you are six-foot-five with a stub, someone in the shower is going to point it out and start everyone making fun of you. If you are the short guy that could be a porn star, there is going to be someone who says, "Holy moly! Hey everyone, look at that thing." Boys don't care about being naked. We are all naked together and start showering together in grade school football. It's just what we do.

I do feel sorry for some black dudes. We have heard the stereotype that they are huge. The fact is, around 90% of all races and ethnicities are in that same range. So, my guess is that there are a lot of black guys who are just average. The black stereotype is so prevalent that every time one of those "average" black guys pulls down his pants, I could almost hear that downward sound a slide whistle makes in the girl's mind. I wouldn't want to have to deal with that expectation. The stereotype is only cool if a guy can back it up. If you're a black guy who is average (90%), the stereotype sucks for you. How many black guys just said, "Preach on, brother, David!"

Even though guys don't care about being naked, make no mistake about it, there is a guy "code" and "rules." When a guy is in the shower, he should keep his head down, shower quick and mind his own business. Unfortunately, old guys forget these rules. There is nothing worse than when an old guy starts talking to me in the shower. I was in the lockers a few weeks ago, sitting on a bench putting on my socks, and this old guy walks right next to me and starts toweling off his shriveled body. He lifted one leg up onto the bench to dry the "boys." What a nightmare . . . one minute I am minding my own business and the next minute I am eye level with an acorn in a cotton field. Seriously, that is what it will look like when I get old? I am an adamant supporter of stem-cell research and cloning.

For the older guys, it is a companionship thing. They want to feel like they are "still in the game" and want to talk about sports, politics, and their workout. I can envision an older guy telling his wife, "So, I was having an interesting discussion with this young fella at the gym." My recap of the encounter was different . . . it was more like "I just saw some old guy's balls!"

Okay, so back to LL Cool J. When I was in high school, I put up a giant poster of LL Cool J on my bedroom wall. I am pretty sure it was the first time a black guy – either living or on a poster- was ever in Seven Hills. My mother asked my dad if I were on drugs and if I had joined a gang. It's funny because Mom failed to grasp the concept that in order to be in a gang, I needed more than one person. I grew up on Cabrini Lane named after the saint, Mother Cabrini. The other streets in my neighborhood are St. Joseph Drive, St. Francis Drive, Calvin Drive, and there is even a Mother Theresa Way. Seriously, what would my gang colors be, Easter purple? Seven Hills is about as "gangster" as Vanilla Ice.

I put the LL Cool J poster up because he was the first rap superstar. Don't ask me how, but I was always into different music. I was a 12-year-old white kid from Seven Hills listening to Midnight Starr, Freddie Jackson, the Dazz Band, Rick James, the Gap Band, Kool and the Gang, George Clinton, Whodini, Run DMC, Slick Rick, the Mary Jane Girls, and everyone else on urban radio. To this day, I still know every word to Grandmaster Flash's "The Message" and the Sugar Hill Gang's "Rapper's Delight," and I probably haven't heard or sung those songs in over a decade.

LL Cool J was my favorite because I loved his swagger. My brother Mark used to take me to concerts, and he took me to see LL Cool J at the now demolished Front Row Theater. This was one of the coolest places for a concert. There were only about 30 rows in the venue – the seats were laid out as a perfect circle and the stage slowly rotated the whole show so everyone had some front time. I had loved LL's first record, *Radio*, but the deal was sealed when *Bad* was released. Even back then, LL Cool J was ripped. Every girl at the show was screaming his name, and he could have had anyone he wanted. I remember thinking, "Wow, he's got a pretty good gig going."

Just then, LL did something I will remember for the rest of my life. As if the women in the crowd weren't in enough of a feeding-frenzy for him, stage hands put a purple, velvet couch on the stage. LL took off the top of his jogging suit revealing his jacked up physique – he placed the microphone on the couch – and laid face down on the couch while still singing "I Need Love." At this point, chaos had broken loose. Women were throwing bras and panties and Lord only knows what else at him. Of course, right on cue, the drum beat kicked in, and LL started humping the couch. There are probably five guys in the world who could make dry-humping a couch look sexy. Clearly, I am not one of them. Clearly, LL Cool J was and is.

I don't know LL Cool J's personal life, but the fact was he could have used his penis more than the rest of us combined back then if he wanted. As if his "I Need Love" performance weren't impressive enough, I saw LL on his next tour at the giant Richfield Coliseum. The hall went black – there was a red siren light flashing throughout the building – the massive stage opened up – and LL drove on stage in a Red Lamborghini or Ferrari convertible singing his classic anthem, "I'm Bad." It was one of the greatest entrances I ever witnessed, and it prompted me to turn to Joe Shumay and say, "He is bad!"

For the confused white folk out there, let me explain: "I'm bad" in the rap world really means "I'm really, really good." I'm so good, you shouldn't mess with me. If I were a boxer coming into the ring for a fight, "I'm Bad" is the song I would play. I'm a gentleman, but play me that song before a fight, and I could whip Mike Tyson. Seeing as though I was the only kid listening to LL Cool J in my "hood" growing up, my friends would love when I would rap to them in the car. LL loves to rap about himself in the third person. So, it was easy to substitute my name "Dave" in the songs in place of "J." For example, I would rap, "I'm the baddest, taking out all rookies, so forget Oreos eat Cool Dave cookies." Deep down, we all have the desire to perform. Of all the dumb things I could be good at, I can rap. Great, what's that going to get me?

Fast forward a couple decades and I met LL Cool J backstage at the Cleveland House of Blues, my favorite place to see a concert. LL Cool J has had a great run. He has transitioned to movies, television, and is still rapping. He is a well-loved brand and more than any other celebrity I know, if I say his name, women are like, "Oh, I love LL – he is so fine – I would do him." I do know that LL Cool J is supposedly religious and happily married, which is a great thing for other guys because no matter how cool a guy thinks he is, his woman would probably sleep with LL Cool J if she had the chance, so I am glad he is out of the competition.

In a great story about life coming full circle, we were backstage at the concert, and I had to use the restroom. So, while I was away, LL came out for the meet and greet. The only people he was meeting were my friends Tim Maffo, Rachel Steck, and me. It is pretty interesting to see but each "band" or performer has varying degrees of people traveling with them. For a band like George Clinton, it is chaos. There are people everywhere with dozens of band members, road crew guys, friends, and a whole other cast of characters. For LL Cool J, he had a total of five people with him. He had a tour manager, his DJ on stage playing the records, and a couple of other guys. His whole crew could probably fit into a Honda, which is smart because that means there are fewer people splitting the check.

While I was at the bathroom, LL Cool J came out and was standing near Tim and Rachel waiting to meet me. Tim overheard him talking to his manager, and he said, "I'm pretty excited and nervous to meet the mayor." Come on, how hilarious is that? LL Cool J, the guy who I worshipped since I was 12 – the guy who taught me to have swagger – was excited to meet me. It was clearly not a thought I would have had when I first hung that poster on my wall that some day he would be excited to meet me. When I think of that story, it makes me smile a little and take pride in what I have done in life. Anyway, whenever Tim tells that story, he can't help but put an "Oh, Jesus" in it at how preposterous it is that LL Cool J was excited to meet me. I don't want to get political, but President Barack Obama ruined my groove a little. You see, before he became the first black President, meeting the mayor in the black community was a big deal. Seriously, of all the encounters I have had, black folk would get the most excited – they genuinely thought meeting the mayor was a big moment. Now, it's not as exciting because the President is black. If anyone on Obama's staff reads this, they need to "hook a brother up" and get me some prime meetings because the President is taking bread off my table.

When I finally came back and met LL, it was exciting. He was jovial, with a giant smile, and muscles in places most of us don't have places. I put my hand on his back and I could feel lumps and rolls of muscles even on his back. LL Cool J is one dude I would never want to make angry.

One of my favorite things about meeting the celebrities is seeing what takes place backstage. Almost as cool as meeting LL Cool J was seeing him take the stage for his concert. When I met LL, I met him way before the concert because he likes to "get in the zone" before the show. When it was time for his concert, his DJ on the "wheels of steel" was playing old hip-hop classics. Again, this is a smart idea. Instead of some crappy opening act that

Mayor David Bentkowski with the godfather of rap, LL Cool J, aka James Todd Smith.

costs money and no one cares about, LL has one guy playing the crowd's favorite songs. It put the crowd in a fun mood. Everyone was singing and dancing. The DJ was on stage. Off stage right (which means the left side) there was one guy behind a massive sound board running all the sound. Tim and Rachel went to get a drink, so at this point it was just me and the sound guy standing backstage. All of a sudden, LL walked down a ramp from his dressing room. He had a sweat suit on and was wearing the hood. It was open and I could see his chest covered with sweat. He looked like he was about to go beat the crap out of Evander Holyfield. For about three minutes, he stood backstage on his own just psyching himself up – bobbing his head – taking little steps back and forth – making little movements of controlled energy. No joke, he probably could have entered the crowd and successfully beat up all 1,000 people in attendance if he wanted. I have never, EVER, seen someone as intense as he was at that moment. All of a sudden, his music kicked in and he stormed onto stage. The place went bananas. Talk about having everyone's attention from the get go? Right out of the gate, he had every single person in the hall pumping a fist, rapping the songs, jumping up and down. It was just an impressive mass of people all doing the same thing, feeding off his energy.

I was at the 2009 Essence Music Festival in New Orleans, and the video screens were flashing various celebrities. Of all the people they flashed, when they flashed LL Cool J, he scored the biggest screams. Yes, "Ladies Love Cool J" – still today. Every celebrity could learn from LL Cool J. I have never read anything bad about him in the tabloids. He has been around for decades. He is always trying new projects, yet he is smart enough to keep doing the things that made us first love him, rap and rock the mic. If I could, I wouldn't mind getting my hands on that original poster. I would like to put it up in a gallery or office. It's a good reminder for me to be a success like LL, and to remember that boyhood dreams of being like your favorite celebrity can come true.

While in New Orleans for the Essence Festival, I was staying with my friends Rachel Hurdle and Beverly Nix Conier. They have a great place on Decatur Street, and I walked to Bourbon Street while they were doing some work. I walked by a bar that was blasting great hip-hop and rap songs from the 1980s and 1990s. I went inside and was the only white person in a crowd of 300. It was sort of like karaoke. There was one singer working for the bar rapping most of the songs, and every now and then he would hand the mic to someone so he could sing. I was standing there in the front row watching all this, and I heard the familiar opening of "I'm Bad." Before the LL rap part started, the song opened with a police officer putting out a fake APB on LL Cool J: "Calling all cars, calling all cars, be on the lookout for a tall, light-skinned brother with dimples, last seen on Farmer's Boulevard heading east, alias LL Cool J . . . he's bad." While that was taking place, the guy with the mic attempted to hand it to a black guy next to me. He didn't know the words and declined. Guess who did know the words? Guess who has known every word of that song for the last 20 years? Yep, LL Cool Dave. I grabbed the mic and told the guy, "I know it!" I hopped on stage and the place went crazy. It was such a rush. I immediately started rapping, "No rapper can rap, quite like I can, I'll take a muscle bound man and put his face in the sand . . . " and I was off and running. I nailed every word. There are such great lyrics in that song. I was taunting and playing with tough guys in the crowd, pointing at them as I rapped "I eliminate punks, cut em up in chunks, you assume to hurt me and your ego shrunk." Picture this scene – some cracker white kid from Seven Hills leading 300 drunk black folk singing "I'm Bad." At one point, I had everyone in the room waiving their hands from side to side and making the "LL" sign with their fingers. The guy singing for the bar took the mic stand and placed it over my shoulders as if knighting me as the king. If anyone has video of this, please send it to me because it was the stuff of legends. When the song was over, I jumped into the crowd, people were hugging me and high-fiving me, and I just walked out of the bar and was walking by myself on Bourbon Street moments later and no one could have ever guessed what had just happened.

LL Cool J and Mayor David; "We're bad!"

My New Orleans trip had some more funk and music to it as I met Charlie Wilson of The Gap Band. Their song "You Dropped a Bomb on Me" was a favorite of mine growing up, and it captured my views about playing basketball. Teammates would joke that if I was in the gym, I considered myself open and I was shooting – dropping bombs. During the Essence Festival, I met Queen Latifah, John Legend, Holly Robinson Peete, En Vogue, Finesse Mitchell, and Al Reynolds. That weekend, the big performers were Beyonce, Al Green and Lionel Ritchie. I would have loved to meet all three of them, but the festival was crazy, even I couldn't work my magic to make it happen.

The only white performer all weekend was singer Robin Thicke, son of television's Allen Thicke. Everywhere I went, people were asking me for autographs and to take pictures because they thought, "Oh, he's a clean-cut white guy. He must be Robin Thicke." Really, black folk, do honkeys all look that much alike?

The strangest meeting for the weekend was meeting New Orleans Mayor Ray Nagin, who was the mayor during Hurricane Katrina. Mayor Nagin was having a party so I put on a stylish outfit thinking it would be some fancy, stuffy official type of event. The party was at a club and looked like the Source Hip Hop Awards. People were pimping, dancing, and partying. For any of my residents who might wonder if my efforts in bringing attention to Seven Hills are a little bit much or outside the box, go hang with Mayor Nagin for a night. Even I was like, "Really, this is the mayor's party? This is crazy!" You know it was a wild time if even I was saying that!

My final memory of New Orleans was hanging with Sarah Ashley Longshore, a brilliant artist who uses a special glazing technique to make her paintings look like porcelain when they are in fact feather-light canvass.

Mayor David Bentkowski and Charlie Wilson of The Gap Band at the Essence Music Festival in New Orleans.

Mayor David Bentkowski with actress Holly Robinson Peete at the Essence Music Festival in New Orleans.

Mayor David Bentkowski and the ladies of En Vogue.

Mayor David Bentkowski and New Orleans Mayor Ray Negin.

"Sugar Daddy" Mayor David Bent-
kowski.

Mayor David Bentkowski with artist
Sarah Ashley Longshore.

My Future Wife, Norah Jones?

Norah Jones is hot. I'm talking so hot she would make me sweat like O.J. on the witness stand. She's hot and tiny, also. I'm pretty sure I could fit her into my shirt pocket. She would be the perfect woman to marry because she could sing at the wedding and stand on the wedding cake at the same time.

Did you ever hear someone ask, "What do you look for in a woman? Are you a leg man? Do you like pretty eyes?" For me, it is all about the face, and Norah Jones has a perfect face. It's hard to quantify, but she has flawless skin that looks like a doll. She has sexy eyes. Again, it's hard to point to one feature, but all together, it just works.

She is so good looking that even if she tries to rough up her look, she still looks awesome. Johnny Depp and Brad Pitt are like that. They are always doing crazy stuff with their hair or looking weird for a movie role and they still look good. Nina Persson from The Cardigans tried this, also. When the band sang "Lovefool," she was a gorgeous long-haired blonde with dimples, perfect teeth, and deep blue pools for eyes. A couple records later, she chopped her hair off, started wearing all black clothes like a biker chick, and tried to look all rough and grunge. She looked even hotter. I met Norah six years after she first arrived on the scene and she dramatically changed her look. She clipped her signature locks and even added wild color to her hair. As you can see in the picture, she's still smoking hot, just in a different way.

Now for the part none of you are going to believe in a million years – I think she thought I was cute when I met her. I'll give you a few seconds to stop laughing... okay... I'll continue.

I broke up with my last serious girlfriend in September of 2008. After being with someone for nearly three years, I wasn't exactly in the mood to find someone new; I was just hanging out with a lot of friends for awhile. After being "David Downer" for a couple of months, my friends were like, "Dude, you have to get your swagger back." Swagger is my favorite word. I have the word framed on my desk. I don't like to be cocky. I don't like to be conceited. I think there is a difference, and I think having a "swagger" is the goal. Daniel Craig as James Bond has swagger. LL Cool J taking the stage at a concert has swagger. As a man, I want to be sexy. As I get older, I want to be the guy that still looks good and dresses sharply, who has confidence, and who acts like he deserves the affection others give him.

While working at a bank during college, once a week a handsome man in his forties would walk into the bank to make a deposit, and the five female tellers would all be squirming in their chairs. What I always remember about that guy is that he was a perfect gentleman. Yes, he was always in a suit with his hair cut short sporting a touch of grey on the sides. He was sexy to these women because he was kind and treated them with respect. I want to be sexy for the right reasons. I want the woman I am with to know that I will always do right by her.

I want to be the guy who walks into the bank and who women "ooh" and "ahh" over – and then act even cooler with that affection by making everyone else feel good. That is confidence. That is class. That is swagger!

By the way, while working at that bank, I set off the dye-pack INSIDE the building, causing the bank to be shut down for a couple days. I have several talents. I am an average lawyer. I am a very good lobbyist. I hope I am a spectacular mayor. And I was probably the worst bank teller in history. I am not a detail kind of guy. I'm an idea guy. The whole concept of numbers . . . and math . . . and balancing every day . . . ugh, is not for me. I hated that job more than I could explain. I only lasted one summer. I would correctly balance my drawer maybe once a week. There would be days when my drawer would have hundreds of dollars extra. Seriously, how could I have hundreds of dollars extra? Now that I think about it, I never recount the money that a teller gives me; some "math wizard" like me could be shorting me every time.

One Saturday morning, the boss told me that I was going to work the drive through window for the first time. Each teller had a drawer that was kept in the vault. I put my drawer in the drive through station and then went to get my dye-pack. A dye-pack is a bundle of $20s that secretly has an ink mechanism inside of it. If I were robbed as a teller, I would put the dye-pack of $20s into the robber's sack and as soon as he hit the front door, there is a field that sets off an explosion of the dye-pack; it explodes and stains all the money, ruining it for the bad guy.

Well, no one told me that there was a field between the main teller area and the drive-through window. I walked to my station holding this dye-pack of $20s and the thing exploded in my hand. I was holding this thing in my hand freaking out – it was smoking red smoke and ink like a safety flare – so I didn't know what to do – so I just whipped it like I was playing "hot potato" . . . wait for it . . . into the bank.

I would pay big money to have the video of this because it had to be hilarious. Picture me effeminately screaming and "whipping" the dye-pack into the main area of the bank. The bank was closed for days because they had to clean the carpets, drapes, walls, and everything else. My boss was this prickly lady way too serious to be working with someone like me and she was furious. Needless to say, they fired me.

A few months after my September relationship break-up, I was ready for something fun and Norah Jones came to town as part of the *Rock the Vote* tour for the 2008 Presidential election just days before the November election. Actually, the concert was in Omarosa's hood, Youngstown, Ohio. It was an amazing concert line-up featuring Norah, Sheryl Crow, and the Beastie Boys. The Beastie Boys have been one of my favorites for decades and the place went crazy when they played "Sabotage." The Beasties were all dressed alike – dancing – and then without anyone knowing – actor Ben Stiller, who had switched places with one of the band members – was dancing on stage – and then took off his hat revealing himself to the crowd. It was a great, great show.

I had wanted to meet both Norah and the Beastie Boys and had it set up with both camps. I'll talk about the Beastie Boys' failed execution later, but as for Norah, everything went as planned. Norah played first, starting early at 7:00 p.m. I was supposed to meet her after her performance. I had seen her several times previously, and I knew she played with her Handsome Band. One of those guys, Lee Alexander, was her boyfriend for a long time. When she took the stage, I was very surprised to see that she had cut her hair super short and that she was with an all-female band. The Handsome Band was gone.

As usual, she was amazing. I would put her voice up against anyone's. There are some people who have a unique voice and amazing talent; Norah is easily near the top of that list. There is no one else like her. Just like there is no one else like Roberta Flack. Just like there is no one else like Billie Holiday or Mahalia Jackson. Norah Jones is voice royalty. She could sing me names out of a phone book, and I would listen to it for hours.

When it comes to meeting celebrities, I normally play it cool. Part of the ruse is that I am supposed to be a big deal; they want to meet me as much as I want to meet them. Funny, I know. For whatever reason, I was caught up in the moment when I met Norah. We were in the tunnel underbelly of the arena and Norah was approaching with her manager. I don't know what possessed me, but I went running up to her and gave her a giant hug. Mind you, this is my first time meeting this person and the second I see her, I am running up to her hugging her. She was probably thinking, "Security!" When I am nervous around a girl, I have "tells" like in poker. A "tell" is a nervous gesture that a person does that lets everyone else know that they are nervous. With Norah, I was going through my entire "tell" playbook. I was talking a million miles an hour. I was saying the same things over and over. I wouldn't shut up, and she couldn't get a word in edgewise.

I finally pulled it together and gave her the proclamation. I just kept blabbering and blabbering on and on about how talented she was and how beautiful she was. A normal meet and greet is about a minute or two. I say hello, take my picture, and I am gone. As for pictures, it is normally one quick snap shot. With Norah, I just kept taking picture after picture with her. We were like high school friends at the end of senior year. We were laughing about our picture good sides, taking pictures from different angles, taking some with the proclamation and some without. The meet and greet was probably a good 15 to 20 minutes. About 15 minutes into the meet and greet, my trusty right-hand-man, Chris Matthews, whispers to me, "Dude, what's going on? You two look like you are newlyweds. You should ask her out."

I said, "Get out of here, it's Norah Jones. She's just being gracious. Besides, she's been dating that Lee guy for years."

Chris said, "All right, you're missing your chance."

I finally stop talking and let the poor woman go. She was sweet and funny, I would have married her on the spot. I had purchased good seats for all of us, but since we were supposed to meet the Beastie Boys after their show, Norah told her manager, "Why don't we put them in the family section so we know where they are, and they can come meet the Beasties easier?" The family section was a completely empty section located on the side and sort of behind the stage. The people on stage had their backs to us. The seats I bought were way better, but these were interesting because I could see the behind-the-scenes action. I could see Sheryl Crow dancing by the sound engineer. I could see Ben Stiller putting on his costume before he duped the crowd. And now for the good part – I could see Norah and her band hanging out after her performance.

Here's where the story gets interesting. The bowl section of seats is permanent – and at Row A, there is about a 10-foot drop to the concrete floor. The venue hall floor is probably a little lower because they may have to install a basketball court, or ice arena, etc. Point being, when people are in the stands, those on the floor are below them. After meeting Norah, we were sitting in our seats and all the girls in her band walked out onto the side stage floor and stood by the sound engineer. Keep in mind, they never met me. They were not at the meet and greet. The four of them were pointing at me smiling, waiving, and giggling. Chris says, "See, I told you, Norah went and told her band about you." A few minutes later, Norah came out and joined her band in waving to me, giggling, and even reciprocated a kiss I blew to her. I am a realist and it was absolutely possible (and likely) that they were just waving to be nice, or the band heard I was the mayor and mistakenly thought that was a big deal . . . whatever. But by golly, how insane would it be if Chris was right and Norah went to her band and said, "Go check out the cute mayor." Just once, God, give me something like that, please! I have never had a pretty girl sit next to me on a plane. Never happens. I get the 400-pound football player who forces me into a fetal position with my face wedged against the window. I've been in what seems like 100 bridal parties. Just once can I have a beautiful, single partner who wants to dance all night? Never happens. In the words of the great Jimmy Buffett, I am going to take Chris' position and tell everyone that Norah Jones liked me – "That is my story and I am sticking to it."

The whole way home, I was excited. When I got home, just out of curiosity, I Googled "Norah Jones relationship status" and there were a bunch

Mayor David Bentkowski with his future wife (in his dreams) singer Norah Jones.

of articles and postings about how Norah Jones had broken up with her boyfriend, Lee Alexander, earlier in the year. WHAT!!!!!!!!!!! As ESPN's Chris Berman would say, "Fum-------bleeeeeeeeeeeeeee!" Norah Jones was single, I met her for 20 minutes, and I didn't make it happen. All together, "David Bentkowski is a dumb ass."

For fun, I put my picture with Norah on my Myspace page and titled it, "Mayor David Bentkowski and his future wife, Norah Jones." Ahh, dare to dream, dare to dream. Norah's "Come Away with Me" is one of my all-time favorite songs. Every time I hear it, I can just close my eyes and smile, thinking of how sweet she was to me. Did she think I was cute? Should I have asked her out? The world will never know. I do know this: I once drove seven hours to New York on the spur of the moment to go help Omarosa on *The Celebrity Apprentice*. You can bet your Polish nose that if Norah Jones called me tomorrow for dinner, I would be in New York faster than you could say – again, all together – "David Bentkowski is a dumb ass."

The "No's" and the "Not So Nice"

The meet and greet with the Beastie Boys never happened. This chapter is going to visit those encounters that fell through as well as some that happened and could have gone a little better. Let me reiterate that I am well aware that meeting me is NOT a big deal. Remember chapter one? The whole point of this book is to make fun of how ridiculous a premise it is that the offer of meeting me works for some people and how I have attempted to use these encounters to promote my beloved city. Also, I am not a mean person. I don't like to talk negatively about people or criticize them, so I am not going to "throw anyone under the bus." Further, as a mayor, I have seen first-hand how actions of people under me can negatively reflect on me without me even knowing about it. Therefore, it would not be fair for me to embarrass a celebrity that might not have even known about my efforts to meet them.

The night I met Norah Jones, I also was supposed to meet the Beastie Boys after their show. The thing I always tell friends about these meet and greets is that it is never a sure thing until it happens. Many things can go wrong. Many times, my fate can be in someone else's hands. I won't throw any of the celebrities under the bus because they might not have even been aware of my existence. There are some basic lessons in public relations and professionalism that some of their staff can learn and these examples will easily demonstrate those lessons.

When the call for the meet and greet is first made, the manager or the band or whoever doesn't owe me anything, can easily decline, and I'll be on my way. There were a handful of bands that I love that did this. I called the band Garbage, singer Beck, and the band Depeche Mode. These are three of my all-time favorites and without hesitation, they said, "Sorry, not interested." I can't be mad at them. For starters, who knows if the band even knew I called. A manager or publicist could have independently decided, "That's not something they would be interested in" or the band just might have a policy of not meeting anyone so the publicist just always gives a blanket no. That's cool, no problem, and life goes on and I'm only out the few minutes it took to make the call. If anything, I appreciate the honesty and saving of my time.

Even though I can't be mad because I don't know the celebrity's role in the no, I will say that if I were famous, I would have a yes policy. Think about it, why would I say no to anyone? The whole point of being famous is to be known and use that popularity to further a career. Fame is fleeting. If I were ever famous, I would meet every person in the world who wanted to meet me. I know this is how I would be because I have been famous on a small scale in Ohio and I have not been annoyed by it. In fact, my fame can be a true test of patience because I have the notoriety without the giant cash rewards or star treatment that big celebrities receive. In my town everyone knows me. When I go to breakfast, all 15 tables in the place have people that know me, say hi, and talk to me while I'm eating. What's the big deal? It is fun! If you are Depeche Mode, fans come up to you saying, "You are awesome." I continually have people coming up to me while eating saying, "Mayor, my sewer is blocked" or "Mayor, when are you going to pave my street?" If you are in a band or a singer, you should accept meet and greets as something that you should do and do them quickly and organized like Gwen Stefani. Instead of making a big production out of it, just have an easy yes policy, have everyone quickly assembled into a big room, give everyone their picture, and be done with it. Gwen Stefani met about 100 people in 10 minutes – what is hard about it? Trust me; in 10 years when a star's fame is over and he is on the *Surreal Life 27*, he is going to beg for people to know him. I judge people based not on what they do, but on how they act while doing it. Remember, being king is only cool if you are a good king and your servants love you. Being famous is only cool if people love you. The best example I can think of is Cleveland's favorite son, Drew Carey. I have a whole chapter about Drew and other Cleveland people coming up, but the short story on Drew is that he is the nicest guy in the world. If you talked to 5,000 people who had met him, 5,000 people would tell you he was awesome and gracious, and they loved him. Someday, Drew might not be on television or in Hollywood.

But, when he comes home to Cleveland, like LL Cool J would say, he'll "get worshipped like an old battleship."

The second reason to be gracious is because the odds of becoming famous are slim. When someone does make it, he needs to run with it as hard as he can for as long as he can. I read a great article about Beyonce Knowles. She is everywhere doing tours, records, movies, selling her clothing line . . . basically anything she can think of doing. In the interview she discussed how she knew fame would not last forever. Beyonce wants to do as much as she can for as long as we love her. She knows it will all end some day; she wants to make as much money and secure as much good will as possible. A star is only at the top for a short time. Think Diana Ross. Think Whitney Houston. Think Brittany Spears. Sure, they still have a slice of the pie, but they were only THE top dog for so long.

While at the New York Book Expo, there was a two-page flier that had tips for promoting a book. One of the things it said was, "Don't think any promotion is too small. You never know what it can lead to in the end." It told the story of some author who said no to a small, local television interview for his book. Some other author said yes to the appearance. Oprah Winfrey's people were doing research and came across the interview, and put the guy who said yes on Oprah's show. The guy who said yes to that one television appearance ended up on Oprah and sold a crazy number of books.

Those who said yes to me are getting a lot of coverage in this book. Who knows how many people will buy this book, but as you can tell, I am usually pretty flattering in what I have to say. It would not be a crazy stretch for 10,000 to 100,000 people to buy this book. If lightning strikes, it could be many more.

I do have a title. I am a mayor and an author and, obviously, a marketing hustler. Don't you think a 30-second picture with me is going to show up in a lot of places? I know college kids who have 4,000 Facebook friends. Yes, Depeche Mode, take a picture with each college kid because he is going to put it on his Facebook page and he is going to tell 4,000 of his friends, "Depeche Mode is the coolest." When a band is trying to make it, members would drive six hours in a small van to play a concert in Poughkeepsie for 20 people. Why not take 30 seconds for a picture that thousands will see? Don't forget your roots. Again, I don't have a problem with those who say no right away, but I just think it is silly to pass up on any opportunity.

What I do have a problem with is broken commitments. For the Beastie Boys I was given specific instructions by some handler. I was told to wait until after the show at the same location I met Norah Jones. My group waited at least an hour. I have done this dozens of times. I know the drill and I know how to avoid various land mines. Sure enough, there was some rent-a-cop security who came along and said, 'You have to leave." Firmly, I stated, "Actually, we are waiting for the tour manager. We were given specific instructions to wait here for a meet and greet." Even though they started clearing out the building, the rent-a-cop let us stay. As time passed by, I finally shouted out to a roadie and asked him to track down our contact. Our contact came out and basically blew us off. His official answer was, "Oh, the band is exhausted from the long tour and isn't meeting anyone tonight." Really? Exhausted? That struck me as funny because I just saw them whooping it up on the side of the stage with Ben Stiller and everyone else and they looked like they were having the time of their lives.

I don't blame the Beastie Boys. I love the Beastie Boys. If I ever have the chance, I will lead a campaign to make sure they get in the Rock and Roll Hall of Fame in Cleveland. What is nonsense is the old "switcharoo." Don't tell me to wait for an hour after the show if the meeting is not going to happen. I have better things to do with my time. Don't give me some line that the band is exhausted when I just saw them partying.

This is a good lesson for anyone in business: pay attention to your workers since their actions could reflect on you. As mayor, we had a new Panera Bread open in my town. We love Panera Bread. The opening was a giant success. They are a great corporate citizen and volunteered to sponsor city events. Imagine how pissed I was when their general manager called me to tell me that one of my firefighters was a jerk during an inspection. Apparently, his idea of welcoming a new business to town was to use aggressive language, talk in a condescending tone, and cause a scene in front of customers. Needless to say, that firefighter and I had a little "pep talk" about his attitude. My guess is the Beastie Boys didn't know I even existed and that's fine. But man, I hate a missed opportunity. Had I met the Beastie Boys, I would have written about 20 pages discussing why I think they are great.

Maybe I'm a control freak, but I would want to be the person who made the decision as to whether or not I wanted to meet someone in a similar situation. The rep or manager who is supposed to be handling those things might not always make the right call. It's great to have handlers and all that, but only I can make the best call for me. Friends will ask me what they should do about a relationship. That is the dumbest thing in the world. When I am in a relationship, I am the only one who was there for every moment. I was there during the happy times, the fights, and the sleeping together. How could anyone else other than me know how I am feeling or what I should do? When I ask someone else or rely on someone else, I am usually looking for someone to justify my desire to leave. Listen, if I were dating a Victoria's Secret model, I wouldn't care what anyone said about her; I'm staying with her. Why would anyone care what anyone else thinks about his relationship?

I also had a near miss with the band Sugar Ray. I have attempted to use these celebrity encounters to promote my city, and my voters in Seven Hills would appreciate the creative ways I have attempted to do this. For starters, I always want to offer these bands the use of our $10 million rec. center. We are about 15 minutes away from downtown Cleveland where most of the concerts are, and life on the road for these bands is terrible. The busses usually have limited bathroom facilities and there is often no laundry. The other thing that is important to celebrities is privacy. Justin Timberlake and his massive road crew are not swimming at the Holiday Inn pool. There would be thousands of screaming girls diving into the water with him. My idea would be to let some of these bands use our rec. center in private. We can get them in and out, no one would know they were there, and they could enjoy a fun day of swimming, playing basketball, showering, lifting weights, and much more. It would be a great few hours to break up the pain of life on the road. If a couple of bands took me up on it; I would hope to get the word out to all traveling acts and start charging big money to the bands for the center's rental. If Justin Timberlake or the Dave Matthews Band wants to bring 200-member crews to the rec. center for a day of fun, the $5,000 I would charge would be doable. It is a creative revenue source for the city for doing nothing more than having a fun day with a big star in town.

The second thing I learned to do is to have celebrities sign items that I donated to charity. These items often were auctioned off to raise money. If Gwen Stefani signed a CD for charity that makes the charity $100, then good for everyone involved.

Third, I have generated a little publicity for being the young mayor. Several celebrities have indicated they had heard of me even before we met. It is great exposure for Seven Hills if they talk about meeting me on their web pages or fan pages. A lot of the pictures for which I have posed have turned up on the internet, and as you can tell, I am always positive about Seven Hills and the good message of our city is spread. I have used some of the celebrity encounters on my television show, and, most importantly, I use the pictures and stories when I guest speak at the local schools. I use my celebrity encounters as a way to encourage kids to get involved in their city or government and show them that young people can approach politics with a different energy. Do you think some old fart mayor is branding his city by putting a video of him with Justin Timberlake on the Internet? No, he's not, but I am. When I talk to the schools, I teach the kids about branding, marketing, networking, image control and how everyone should do these types of things whether for a city, their business, or their own lives.

When I started meeting celebrities, I never had visions of writing a book. Now writing is another way I will use my encounters to promote my city. I bet you know more about Seven Hills and my leadership style now that you have read this, right? I never knew how something could develop. My instincts were right from the beginning: meeting celebrities could only be a good thing for Seven Hills.

As for Sugar Ray, I made contact with the manager and offered the use of our rec. center for the band. On the day before, the manager was all about it. He made it seem like the rec. center visit was a great idea and he was going to get back to me with a time. The next day, I didn't hear from him and finally texted him again. He replied and said the rec. center visit was not going to happen, and then he asked me if I am the Mayor of Cleveland. "No, I am not the Mayor of Cleveland. I clearly stated that I am the Mayor of Seven Hills. I invited you to verify my identity on my Facebook page, which is filled with Seven Hills' materials. Now that you are backtracking from the meet and greet because you think I am the mayor of some lesser city, you are offending me." My friends Patrick and Brittany Bittel were going to the concert with me. We already had tickets because Patrick works for Clear Channel Communications and gets them for free. We went to the show, and I texted the manager again about the meet and greet, and he said it was not going to happen.

Needless to say, I was not amused. I had three friends with me who were excited to meet Sugar Ray. The manager put me in an embarrassing spot. He said it would happen. I relied on what he said and made arrangements for my friends and me to be there at a certain time. Never one to give up, the band was having a meet and greet after the show if fans bought their new CD. Since I always make good on my promises, I bought us all CDs to meet the band. We stood in line with everyone else and finally met the band. When I finally met the band and gave them their proclamations, they were thrilled. We did not have any proclamation paper in the office, so I personally made each band member one at home. It included a band picture, their individual names and accomplishments, and I made one for EACH band member to keep. Imagine you are the drummer. After awhile, you are going to get pretty upset that everyone keeps giving stuff to lead singer Mark McGrath. Be thoughtful in life and always remember everyone. They all contributed their talent to the bigger picture of Sugar Ray, and they all deserved to be recognized. Maybe they were good actors, but I have seen a lot of people's reactions to a proclamation, and the entire band seemed genuinely appreciative. It even made me feel good that it meant something to them.

While we were waiting to meet them, I asked the tour manager if we could take a picture with the band. He said, "Just you, Mayor." Really? Are you serious? Do you think I would stiff my friends like that? We were at the end of the line. There were only a handful of people left. I'm the mayor with my group whom you stiffed before, after saying yes. Really, you just want me in the picture? Use your head!

Thankfully, the minute we had the meet and greet with the band, it was lead singer Mark McGrath that said, "Hey, Mayor, thank you so much for the proclamation. Let's get a picture with your whole group." The picture had eight people in it. Tour manager says no for whatever reason . . . entire band says, yes. Maybe the normal policy is for the tour manager to say no. Maybe behind closed doors the band says, "We don't want to be bothered with pictures." Who knows? If that is the case, then the tour manager did his job. For many of these celebrities, I have a feeling they want to meet the fans. I have a feeling they want to feel the love and keep the promotion wheel rolling along. If you are a celebrity reading this, maybe this is a talk you should have with your handlers. Are you sure your wishes are being executed? A lot of times a tour manager is a friend. If I were a rock star, my friend Chris would be my tour manager. Chris knows I love meeting people, and he would let everyone in the building meet me. But sometimes, a tour manager is a jack-of-all trade. Maybe he is great at handling day-to-day details. Maybe he is the money guy. Maybe he serves more of a security function. It again illustrates the point that if you have people working for you, it is wise to make sure they are representing you in the way you want to be represented. If the band doesn't know I exist and want a visit, they might be missing out on something they might have wanted to do. They are on the road in a crowded bus going from city to city. After their high-energy show, I would think they want to wind down and enjoy their fans' affections. If they were willing to do a meet and greet and sign CDs, is it too much of a stretch to think they would be up for a picture with the mayor who offered you tremendous hospitality and told you he was going to write good things about everyone in a book? Be a tour manager who knows when to make it happen. In fairness to the tour manager, he very well may have been executing the band's policy. If so, then there should be a clear no protocol from the get go and there should not be the "switcharoo" because you think I am from some small city. I guess it comes down to an issue of judgment. I have seen cops give an 85-year old granny a ticket for something weak like rolling a stop sign. Is scaring granny the goal? Really, is business so slow that we are on 85-year-old granny patrol? If a resourceful mayor calls the record company, tracks down the agent, secures the tour manager's email, sends him a request, offers the use of the rec. center and proclamations . . . and that tour manager initially says, yes, plans on visiting the rec. center, then cancels the rec. center, then cancels the meet and greet . . . and then sees the mayor and his group in line for the meet and greet after they buy CDs, at what point does the little light go off in the tour manager's head that says, "Maybe I should make the group picture happen at this point?" Someone, please, put me in charge of something like this. Make me the tour manager, and I will execute on every detail and our tickets and CD sales will explode as I incorporate every creative marketing strategy known to man. I have seen dozens of these people in action and I would never make a mistake as to what should or should not happen. I would ensure that every person who ever was within 100 feet of my client walked away as his biggest promoter based on that encounter. Mark McGrath and Sugar Ray were excellent performers and they seemed like fun guys. I added Mark McGrath on Facebook the day after to send him the pictures. He kindly accepted and sent me a great note again thanking me for the proclamations and about grabbing a beer the next time he was in town. Dude, of course! However, a few days later, I noticed he dropped me as a Facebook friend. I'll have to ask him what that was all about, but my guess is that I have so many Facebook friends that it gets annoying because every time someone posts something on my page, it shows up on other home pages and there is always a ton of stuff. By the way, if you are on Facebook, only post important stuff. No one cares that you are "tired" or that you reached level 12 on some game. During Easter, there was some dumb game where people would find and hide "eggs" on my page. I would get 100 messages a day that "Mary" found an egg on my page. Ugh, stop it. You should use Facebook to post pictures, let people know if you are going out someplace where they could meet you, let them know about special events or concerts, etc. I have so many friends and get so many updates it is becoming worthless because there is too much to scroll through to find the good stuff. I am mad that Mark McGrath got rid of me because he was Facebook friends with Heather Locklear, and I would have loved for him to make an introduction for me.

As for other meet and greets, I have had some no's by my own design. My friend Tim loves country music, and he wanted me to try to meet Taylor Swift. Sorry, Tim, the mayor is not calling up asking for a meet and greet with a 16-year-old. I don't want Chris Hansen walking in on us and putting me on *Dateline*. My friend Rachel wanted to meet the boy-band, Hanson. Really, Rach? I'm going to call up and say, "Hi, I want to meet Hanson." Why don't I give Zac Efron a proclamation and tell him he's "dreamy" while I'm at it. Ironically, the Hanson brothers are talented artists who write their own songs, play their own instruments and sing live in concert – but the fact remains they sang "MmmBop" and no grown man is ever allowed to admit that he likes like Hanson. I don't make the rules, I just follow them. Check

Friends Patrick and Brittany Bittel join Mayor David Bentkowski with the band Sugar Ray..

out "Penny and Me" – great Hanson song. Chris Matthews is a music snob and hates anything popular or commercial. He likes stuff none of us have ever heard. I am always telling Chris no because he wants to meet bands that he could walk up to on stage and meet because there are only 10 people at the show. I always tease him, "If you want to meet a band, just offer to help them load their equipment into their van after the show." What everyone fails to realize is that even though these meet and greets are fun, I am essentially working. I am very selective in choosing who I meet because when I meet them I am thinking about how I can incorporate this meeting into some positive outcome for Seven Hills. Truth be told, there probably would be value in meeting Taylor Swift or Hanson for charity items or a rec. center rental. But, it is just a lot of work for me to make it happen, and I am trying to be more selective.

The last wrinkle is that out of all the celebrities I have met only a few seemed annoyed by the meeting. Let me again iterate that I know they are doing me the favor. I don't mean to speak ill of them because, after all, they did agree to meet with me. I always like to look at things from a marketing and promotion perspective. I am just fascinated why someone would go through the trouble of meeting someone, and then make it less than perfectly positive in any manner.

Flea from the Red Hot Chili Peppers is probably the greatest bass player in the world. Trivia: Did you know that was Flea playing in Young MC's "Bust a Move" video? It is an all-time classic beat. The Chili Peppers played a concert in Cleveland near Halloween and the band was dressed in costumes. Flea opened the show by coming out of the ceiling dressed like a flea suspended above the crowd on a cable. Trust me, it was awesome. The dude was 100 feet above everyone, jamming away. After the show, we were supposed to meet the band. Right away, they told us that lead singer Anthony Kiedis split and went back to the hotel. We were standing in the hallway in the underbelly of the arena waiting to meet Flea. For those of you who think you could sneak backstage, the answer is, in most places, you can't. There are multiple security checkpoints and guards. Everyone in those hallways or that area is there for a reason. We were standing there for about 30 minutes, and I could hear people on the crews' radios saying, "Who are the lurkers outside the dressing rooms?" Our contact answered, "Oh, they are waiting to meet Flea – it's cool." Moments later, Flea came into the hallway wearing a towel. If you are Chili Pepper fans, you know lack of clothing is nothing new for the band. They used to play concerts wearing only a tube sock placed over special areas. We were told not to bother him and that eventually he would stop and talk to us. We just stood there, and stood there, and stood there waiting for him. It sounds stupid and trust me, we felt stupid. We were just standing there with Flea walking back and forth right past us multiple times. We were just going to leave – I figured I had nothing to lose –I finally just stopped him and said, "Excuse me, Flea, can we get a quick picture?" Should I have said Mr. Flea? He says, "All right, but hurry up, I don't have time for this." I sound like a broken record in this chapter, but again, "If you don't want to do the meet and greet, fine, don't do it." But when your people say "It's cool," and we follow our orders and stand there for 45 minutes, try to be a little more chipper about it. If I were the celebrity, the minute I saw people standing in the hallway, I would take the picture and get rid of them. I can assure you, we didn't want to stand there that long, either. Since Flea was taking the picture, he should have enjoyed the encounter and made it a positive one. Be cool for five seconds and I'll tell everyone Flea rocks. Act bothered and annoyed, and I have to write the above paragraph. PR, folks, PR!

The only other so-so encounter I had was with Cleveland Indians pitcher and baseball Hall of Famer Bob Feller. Before I write another word, I acknowledge that Bob Feller is baseball royalty. He's Bob Feller! For the kids reading this, Bob Feller is a big deal in baseball history. I know this and don't mean any disrespect to him. For a charity luncheon, the Indians would assign one current player or legendary player to a table of 10. It's a cool concept. Pay $50 that goes to charity, and donors get to have lunch with someone. I was absolutely thrilled when Bob Feller sat down at our table. He's Bob Feller! Everyone else at the table was just as excited as I. As soon as Bob Feller sat down, he started telling baseball stories. This was like a dream come true hearing about the "old" days from Bob Feller. When he started, all nine other people at the table were hanging on his every word. Bless his heart, Bob liked to tell stories. After about 15 minutes of stories, I noticed a couple of the other people at the table had left Bob and were having their own conversations. After a couple of more minutes, a few more have jumped ship. I finally realized what was happening – everyone was teaming up with someone to have a conversation so they could jump ship. I was sitting right next to Bob, and I was more screwed than Jack at the end of *Titanic*. By the way, couldn't Rose move her fat ass over on that giant piece of wood so they

both could survive? Maybe I'm a nerd, but I didn't think Bob's stories were too bad. I love baseball and thought he was giving a once-in-a-lifetime perspective. Apparently, everyone else at the table thought otherwise because they all left our conversation and it was just me listening to Bob Feller talk baseball. By the way, this reminds me of something my mother once did to me at a wedding. She called me over to her and some woman and said, "David, you remember Aunt Edna" and then

Mayor David Bentkowski and Flea from the Red Hot Chili Peppers.

Mayor David Bentkowski with Hall of Fame pitcher Bob Feller.

mom walked away. My mother, the sweetest woman God ever made, did the oldest trick in the book, the handoff, and I was stuck talking to Aunt Edna for 30 minutes. "No, Mom, I have no idea who Aunt Edna is. In fact, you don't know who Aunt Edna is, either. In fact, she's not even our aunt. She is just one of those people that everyone calls aunt but she is not related to anyone. Come to think of it, no one at the wedding knew who she was either. She could have been a waitress for all we knew and you dumped her on me for 30 minutes." Revenge will be sweet, mother dear, revenge will be sweet!

Bob Feller's storytelling wasn't the weird part of the encounter. The weird part was that after listening to Bob Feller's stories for 30 minutes the event was over; as everyone was standing up, I asked my new BFF Bob if he would take a picture with me. Swear to God, he initially balked at the request. WHAT? I just listened to some story about you on a farm in Iowa or Kansas or somewhere for 30 minutes and you won't take a picture? Bob's wife, who probably had heard the same stories a handful of times before, said, "Bob, just take the picture with the kid." He did and I like my Bob Feller picture. I like it because some day, I'm going to be telling some little whippersnapper like me some stories, and I will remember and laugh.

At the same Indians luncheon, I spent 10 minutes talking to All-Star catcher and first baseman, Victor Martinez. The entire time I was talking to him, he was just smiling and nodding his head. When he left, Chris said to me, "Are you sure he speaks English?" This was a few years back so the answer was, "I'm not sure." I have heard him do interviews recently, but a lot of these Latin players understand very little when they first arrive in the big

leagues. This was proof for all of my friends that argue that I talk too much, and I don't let others speak. It is quite possible I had a 10-minute conversation with someone who might not have understood a word I was saying. Well, at least he was agreeable.

Mayor David Bentkowski with all-star baseball catcher Victor Martinez.

Hollywood Royalty – Kevin Costner, Bob Hope, Halle Berry, Will Smith and Giovanni Ribisi

I love music, as you can tell. Being a live entertainer has to be one of the greatest feelings in the world. However, as cool as music is, there is nothing better than being a Hollywood movie star. Could you imagine a better gig? You could make $20 million for a few weeks of work. Since the beginning of Tinsel Town, there has always been something magical about movie stars. You wouldn't think living in Cleveland, Ohio, would bring a lot of stars my way, but I have had a pretty good run.

The first movie star I met was about as big as one could get: Bob Hope. Mr. Hope was in Cleveland to visit the old Cleveland Municipal Stadium before they tore it down to build the new Jacobs Field. (Two notes: for starters, you will notice that I refer to him as Mr. Hope. Some people are so big and important to American culture they deserve extra special reverence. Mr. Hope is one of those people. Second, Jacobs Field was the new ballpark for my beloved Cleveland Indians. It is now called Progressive Field, but for those of us who lived and died with the team in their 1990s heyday, it always will be Jacobs Field. The field was named after Indians owner Dick Jacobs, who was arguably the team's greatest owner.) I was working in downtown Cleveland. I just happened to be walking through the Renaissance Hotel and there was this hustle and bustle near the beautiful hotel fountains. I walked over to the crowd and there he was: Bob Hope. Mr. Hope was up in years at this point and at first I thought, "He seemed kind of aloof." He was just standing there as people were snapping pictures like crazy while handlers were giving him instructions, almost talking to him like he was a five-year-old. I happened to be wearing a Cleveland Indians hat and as he was escorted past me, he stopped his whole group, reached out his hand for mine, and said, "Cool hat, kid." When I thought about his contribution to this great country of ours, I realized just what an honor it was to meet him. Even though it was brief, that moment will be etched in my mind forever. Thank you, Mr. Hope, and rest in peace.

Probably the next biggest star I ever met was Kevin Costner. Mr. Costner (yep, Mr. Costner) reminds me of my dad for several reasons. For starters, Mr. Costner is very handsome. I'm straight, but I understand why women go crazy for him. As I've said before, I hope to be distinguished, handsome, sophisticated and all those other fancy adjectives when I am older. Mr. Costner, George Clooney, Brad Pitt, Sean Connery, LL Cool J – there are just some guys who have some kind of spell over women. The amazing thing is that age goes out the window with these guys and fans of theirs. When I told some young girlfriends in their twenties that I was meeting Mr. Costner, they swooned like I was meeting some young male Calvin Klein model. The guy is 30 years older than these women, and they would take off their clothes for him in about 10 seconds.

With his charm and rugged manliness, Mr. Costner reminds me of that image people have of a dad. It's sort of like the Marlboro Man meets the Old Spice guy. My dad, Vic, is a guy's guy as well. He did all those things a dad was supposed to do. He worked hard at his job. He took me to all the places a dad was supposed to take a kid like amusement parks and baseball games. In fact, one of our trips would make for another funny video.

Even when I was young, I was different from the other kids. I was quirky, sort of nerdy, and because I was the "oops" baby five years after my closest sibling, I was my parents' "special little guy" who was sheltered and fawned over. Since my brothers and sister were much older, it was almost like I was an only child because they were off doing their own teen things when I was still in the little kid age. Therefore, my mom and dad would alternate who was watching me, so that meant dad and I had a lot of father/son outings.

One such outing will go down in the Comedy Hall of Fame. When you think Sea World, you probably think Orlando or San Diego. Don't ask me how, but there was also a Sea World 20 minutes from our house, in the town of Aurora. Really, someone thought Aurora, Ohio, was the best place to build a Sea World? Why don't we build a water-park in Alaska while we are at it? Apparently, it was a good idea because it was a success for a long time.

It was located next to Geauga Lake, which was an awesome amusement park loved by many until it couldn't compete with Sandusky's Cedar Point, which is the greatest amusement park in the world, especially if you love death-defying roller coasters.

Once a year my dad would take me to Sea World. Every now and then he would get caught up in being "Joe Dad" and try and do something special. Sometimes it was great, sometimes it was not. This time, it was not. This time, he went up to the Sea World employee, without my knowledge, and said, "Hey, I want my kid to be the kid that kisses Shamu the Killer Whale." For those of you who know me, you are already laughing because even when I was a kid, you know this is one of the last things on earth I would ever want to do. I don't like danger or excitement of any kind. Remember, I don't even know how to swim. You will never read about me dying in some stupid way because I have this bizarre practicality when it comes to my physical well-being. You will never see me bungee-jump, skydive, snorkel – whatever – I will never try any of it. Plus, I know the minute I did try it, I would be the idiot who died doing it. I can just hear my friends saying, "What the heck was David doing rock climbing? He hates exercise."

I say, let all the adventurers who get into danger and trouble die. Seriously, if you are some dope caught in an avalanche climbing a mountain, I say "Oh, well, that will teach you." Every year, there is someone in a hot air balloon or a guy in a raft made out of beer cans who tries to circle the globe. Christopher Columbus was enough – there are no more days to dedicate to holidays –just stop it already. Why are my tax dollars and the lives of smart people being risked to save these folks? Go watch the Discovery Channel instead.

I also don't understand why people continually want to have animal adventures. Did you ever watch the show *When Animals Attack*? Come on, you know you laughed a little when those tigers attacked Siegfried and Roy. You know that tiger was sitting there thinking one day, "How many times is this asshole going to make me do this trick?"

I was not about to be on the next *Attack* video when I met Shamu. I know he was trying to be thoughtful, but seriously, Dad, what part of "I want my kid to be the kid who kisses Shamu the Killer Whale" sounds like a good idea? Perhaps he was forgetting that they call it a "KILLER" whale! Every now and then there is some story about some trained animal that goes nuts and eats someone. Of course, they are going to go nuts and eat someone. They are wild animals! Why am I the only person who understands this? It is a 6,000-pound killer whale. When Shamu goes to kiss me and eats me instead, what the heck is anyone going to do about it? Ground him? Send him to his room? "Bad, Shamu, bad Shamu. No fish for you tonight." You think Shamu gives a crap? Shamu used to swim in the ocean and hook up with more whales than my frat buddies. How ticked off is Shamu that he is in some little tank in Aurora, Ohio? I saw *Free Willy* and that thing can get out if it wants.

Shamu Stadium holds about 2,000 people. My dad arranged it so we were sitting in the front row. This should have been his first red flag that this was a bad idea because I was crying that I wanted to sit in the last row and not the first row. In my crazy, what-could-go-wrong-will-go-wrong, seven-year-old mind, I was thinking the tank would break and I would drown or get trampled, I would get wet, I would somehow fall into the tank, etc. I was balking at this whole concept right out of the gate. Lord only knows if my dad gave the guy some money to make all this happen, but my guess is he did because he was going to try and make this happen whether I wanted it to or not.

The show started and one of those – how do I say this nicely – flamboyant (think TGIFridays waiters) announcer guys started hamming it up with the crowd. He was asking, "Who wants to kiss Shamu?" Of course, 1,999 people were cheering and raising their hands. I was burying my head into my dad's side making sure not to make eye contact with anyone. The announcer came over to me and said, "How about you, young man?" At this point, not only is my head buried in my dad's side, I am pulling his shirt to cover the sides of my face. The announcer thought this is a funny moment and said to the crowd, "Ohh, he's being shy. Let's make some noise for him" and started everybody clapping and cheering for me. "Hey, douche bag, do I look like the type that gives into peer pressure?" If I was 17 and not seven, I would have beaten this guy into a bloody pulp. He grabbed my arm and said, "Okay, let's go kiss Shamu; everyone's watching." I kicked him in the leg and ripped my arm out of his grip. The crowd was laughing – Dad was not. Dad said, "You're embarrassing me . . . just do it." Ahh, yes, "just do it" – the classic Nike phrase. Dad was right, I should take matters into my own hands and "just do" what I wanted to do. With that, I broke free from both of them and ran out of Shamu Stadium. Picture 1,998 (not me or Dad) seated people laughing as this little kid ran away. By the way, I was very fast and I was gone. I wasn't stopping for anyone. The people working the doors smartly got out of my way because I would have run over them like Jim Brown. My dad finally found me about a half-hour later enjoying something much more my speed. I was watching the hot Asian pearl divers. Now, that was an attraction! They put hot Asian women in white bikinis and have them dive in a little tank and pull up oysters for people to see if there are pearls in them. I may have only been seven, but my instincts knew that was a much better time than kissing the killer whale. Dad, sweet thought for trying to hook me up with the special moment that the other kids didn't get, but come on - you have to know your kid better than that. Deep down he just had to know it wasn't happening without a fight.

Of course, every father and son who has ever seen *Field of Dreams* starring Mr. Costner understands the unique bond the two have together. It is completely different than the bond between a mother and son. The mother and son bond is about loving and feeling and nurturing. The bond with dad is quiet and about respect and discipline and loyalty. To this day, I would enjoy "having a catch" with my dad because he is the one who first taught me how to throw a baseball. The dichotomy is amazing. For Mother's Day, I could never buy my mother enough. Dads get an ugly tie or some Old Spice. It's not that people don't love or appreciate their dads; it is just different and less emotional.

Come to think of it, being a dad can be a thankless job. Dads have to do the crap no one else wants to do. Even if my dad and I were mad at each other for something, he was still the go-to guy for certain stuff. Having car trouble? Call Dad. Need to borrow cash? Call Dad. Get in trouble at school? Get your butt beaten by Dad. He was the disciplinarian, the enforcer, and the steady ship in times of trouble. If I was in a Mexican prison and needed $10,000, Dad was the guy I'd call. Mom would come through with the $10,000 as well, but having to hear her yell at me for being in a Mexican prison wouldn't be worth getting out. It would be worse torture than the cell.

My dad was very handsome when he was young. There is this picture of him standing on a diving board when he was on vacation with my mom. His arms are lifted up in diving form; he has six-pack abs and a fifties buzz-

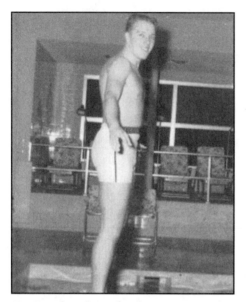

Vic Bentkowski on his honeymoon in the Catskills. Look at that flat stomach!

cut. To this day, even though he is close to 70, I can see that he had it and still has some of it. He still has a full head of hair. He still has young skin. He has a belly, but otherwise has skinny legs and arms. I always yell at him that if he tried now, he could still be dashing like Mr. Costner and look about 40. The other thing I like about my dad is that he never once cheated in any way, shape or form on my mother. My dad wouldn't even think about doing it. Everyone has good and bad qualities but again, I give him credit for being a guy's guy. He is a real man who does things based on principle.

I thank both my parents for giving me what I believe to be a good moral compass. I am old fashioned. I do things because they are right. I love that whole concept of Superman with "good beating evil" and having character and decency and honor. Remember the Kenny Rogers song "Coward of the County?" The gist of the song is that Tommy promised his dad he would never get into a fight because the trouble wasn't worth it. In the song, the "Gatlin boys came calling" and "took turns" with Becky, Tommy's wife. When Tommy went to engage the Gatlin boys, they started laughing as Tommy turned and walked away from them. But as the song says, "You could have heard a pin drop, when Tommy stopped and locked the door." When someone disrespects a guy's woman or does anything to harm someone he loves, a man steps up and does what he has to do. By the way, don't you love Kenny Rogers?

Of course, this could lead to getting your butt kicked, but it is what a guy has to do. Case in point, I was on a date at a local restaurant that had a bar and pool tables. Not my normal type of hangout, but joining us was my date's sister-in-law and her brother. The sister-in-law had just had her first baby and hadn't been to someplace "fun" in nearly a year. This was her first night out since she had the baby. She didn't want to go to a party bar. She thought this restaurant/bar/pool combo would be a good way to tip-toe back into the fun scene. We were just minding our business playing pool, and this guy three times my size was smoking right near the sister-in-law. Mind you, it is illegal to smoke inside a building in Ohio; no mistake about it, the guy was in the wrong. Really soft, the sister-in-law said, "I'm so sorry, I hate to bother you, but I just had a baby and this is my first time out in a year. If it's not too much trouble, could you try not to blow your smoke near us?" Seriously, she said it that nicely.

The guy says, "Don't #%$*ing tell me what to do!" I have never been in a fight in my life. I'm a lover, not a fighter. I probably wouldn't even know how to make a fist to throw a punch without breaking my thumb. I don't know what possessed me, but with the deepest voice I could use, I said, "HEY! You don't talk to a lady like that." Now, 99 out of 100 times, most guys at this point would feel like a jerk and apologize to the lady. Not this guy. It suddenly dawned on me that this guy is trashed drunk and looking to fight. Great, this is the one guy out of 100 who wants to throw down. The guy got in my face and said, "What are you going to do about it?" With all the swagger and confidence I could muster (if I had water in my bladder I probably would have wet myself), I pulled out my wallet, which has my gold safety director's badge, and I flashed him the badge and said, "Punk, I'm not the guy to talk to like that." The guy immediately started apologizing, saying, "I'm sorry, I don't want any trouble." You're damn right you don't want any trouble! I'll whoop you like Reagan whooped Mondale. (Kidding, I think my heart is still racing a little from the concept of my imminent butt whooping). The guy walked away, and everyone in my group started screaming and saying, "Oh, my God, that was awesome" and blah, blah, blah. I'm like, "Will you shut up before he realizes a Girl Scout could beat me up?" and comes back. Remember, it is even cooler if you act like you have already done it.

Make no mistake about it, that dude would have kicked my tail. By the way, how funny is it that the safety director's badge worked? I normally never flash or use the thing. I made no representations that I was any type of law enforcement official. If he took two seconds to read that it said "safety director," he probably would have beaten me up even harder.

Ironically, the badge is gold because I am "management." Normally, a chief or lieutenant gets a gold badge while the rank and file officers have a silver badge. As mayor and safety director, I am technically higher than every one of my safety officers. I hire and fire the chiefs; if it went down in my town, I would be the person in command. Of course, I'm not crazy and in an emergency would do whatever my chiefs advised me to do. What do I know about law enforcement or fire safety?

Standing up to a bully is something my dad or Mr. Costner would do. As for meeting Mr. Costner, it was very exciting. Again, I know celebrities are just people, but hey, Kevin Costner is Kevin Costner. He starred in *JFK, Bull Durham, The Bodyguard, Tin Cup, Field of Dreams, The Untouchables, No Way Out, and Robin Hood*. Need I say more? Meeting him was a pretty good weeknight in Cleveland. He has that "it" factor that, when he walks into a room, he owns it. Sure enough, I could almost feel the women in the room gushing upon his arrival. I'm no Brad Pitt, but even I got a hot date when the night consisted of meeting Kevin Costner. The tour manager introduced us to Mr. Costner as "the mayor and his assistant." Mr. Costner smoothly said to my date Nicole, "You must be the after-hours assistant?" Hey, Mr. Costner, don't be hitting on my lady friend. You might *Dance with Wolves* but any man who made a play for my woman was going to "dance with my fists." For the record, Mr. Costner was a perfect gentleman and didn't hit on my girl. He did make the "after-hours assistant" joke, and I told my date that I thought he was hitting on her just so she could have a great story that Mr. Costner thought she was hot. Trust me, I was there: Mr. Costner could get any woman he wanted. He didn't need to hit on a guy's girl. He was in town singing with his country band Modern West and they were surprisingly entertaining. He reminded me of Jimmy Buffett. He sang six-string music with catchy beats and lyrics and told great stories between songs. It was almost like being at a campfire with someone's cool dad – or my cool dad.

When I met a celebrity of prestige like Mr. Costner, I wondered what my fellow mayors were doing. As of this writing, the Mayor of Cleveland is an honorable man named Frank Jackson. He is a quality public servant, soft-

Mayor David Bentkowski with Oscar-winning actor Kevin Costner.

spoken, and quiet. Critics say he is "not exciting" and has no big visions. Supporters will say he has tried to stop Cleveland's bleeding and has attempted to slow down the city's cash burning and refocus on the basics. He implemented hiring freezes, made some tough cuts, and focused on the daily life of people living in the city versus the exciting projects of other mayors. One of Cleveland's most exciting mayors was Mayor Mike White. He was the complete opposite of Mayor Jackson. Mayor White was more like me. He was always onto the next big project. He was an ideas guy. He built the Rock and Roll Hall of Fame and Museum, Jacobs Field, and the Great Lakes Science Center. Critics said he was a dictator doing it only his way. Supporters like me think he realized he had to be a strong leader and make things happen and ruffle a few feathers along the way if it meant getting things done. Mayor Jackson and Mayor White are both good men – they just have totally opposite styles.

All kidding aside, Mayor Jackson should hire someone like me. He doesn't like the spotlight, and he is about as exciting as drying paint when he talks. Did you ever see the show *Spin City*? I could be Mayor Jackson's right-hand man, like the Michael J. Fox character, Mike Flaherty. Cleveland could be a dynamic, amazing city but one of its biggest downfalls is a defeatist attitude. Let me do the visible projects that Mayor White did. Let me show everyone how to have swagger and remind them of all the good Cleveland has to offer. Even though I think Mayor Jackson means well, was there a good reason why he wasn't there with me meeting Mr. Costner, or Halle Berry, or Will Smith? Mr. Costner is an enterprise. Mr. Costner makes movies that cost hundreds of millions of dollars. Mayor Jackson should have been at Mr.

Costner's concert kissing his tail trying to convince him to do a movie in Cleveland. At a minimum, the public relations component is huge. Mayor Jackson, meet and entertain Mr. Costner when he is in town so when he is on David Letterman's show the following day, he says, "Just had a great stop in Cleveland. Great town, friendly people, met the mayor, blah, blah, blah." If I owned the $20 million XYZ Company and I was coming to town, the mayor, city council, and a bunch of other people would be tripping over themselves to kiss my butt. They would offer me tax credits to bring my company to Cleveland, they would wine and dine me, and they would sell me their city. Mr. Costner spent $200 million on the movie *Waterworld* – why is no one other than me giving him the hard Cleveland sell? Why can't someone more important than me have a light go off in his head and say, "Mr. Costner, Cleveland's economy is struggling; we could use a profitable project such as your next movie to film in the city. We could use the influx of cash and jobs." Can anyone else think of a business that brings $200 million to the table and only is in town for six months?

I'm not stupid and I am going to pimp my city any chance I can get. Mr. Costner and anyone reading this, "Come to Seven Hills and we will make things happen for you." If Mr. Costner wants to film *Waterworld* 6 in Seven Hills, I'll flood the entire city because cash is king and I have to put myself in a position for big things to happen for my city.

Another big star is Will Smith. He is one of the most loved stars in the world. He came to Cinemark Theaters in Valley View, five minutes from Seven Hills, to premier one of his new movies. The studio picked a handful of locations across the country to have a red-carpet premier. Cleveland/Valley View was one of the lucky chosen ones. I was at the premier. LeBron James was at the premier. Will Smith was at the premier. You know who wasn't there? Mayor Jackson. Mayor, what could you possibly have been doing that was more important than meeting Will Smith in your city for this once-in-a-lifetime movie premier? Not only was the mayor not there, he sent his assistant to give Will Smith . . . drum roll . . . wait for it . . . a proclamation. The only thing dumber than a proclamation from me is having the Mayor of Cleveland's ASSISTANT give one. As I watched from the crowd, all I could think was, "You have got to be kidding me?" It was embarrassing. Hey, Will Smith, we want to show how glad we are that you came to

Cleveland by sending a junior assistant to give you this crappy proclamation. Think, people, think! Put me in charge of the Will Smith event. Let me entertain him and his crew for a couple of hours and he'll be writing another song about Cleveland instead of "Miami." For the record, I just shook Will Smith's hand and didn't score a picture with him because LeBron arrived just as Will was getting to me on the red carpet. Will and LeBron played "catch up" and went inside. LeBron, you owe me some courtside seats for ruining my Will Smith meeting. Trivia: I was the tournament director for a basketball tournament called "Fast Break on the Lake" at the Cleveland State University Wolstein Center. Lebron James was a junior in high school and I helped run a tournament where his Akron St. Vincent/St. Mary's team played. As one of my duties, I tried to convince a bunch of local companies to sponsor the event. Dozens and dozens of those dumb asses passed on the event because they never heard of LeBron. I have a copy of the St. Vincent/ St. Mary's sports program with LeBron as a sophomore. People might see even more of LeBron at Cinemark because the Cleveland Cavaliers just built their practice court in Independence, right next door to Seven Hills and Valley View.

Cleveland's own Halle Berry also came to the same Cinemark for her movie release. It's Halle Berry, people. She is one of our greatest exports. She is easily one of the most beautiful women in the world and has won an Academy Award. Send everyone. Have oiled muscle guys in loincloths carry her around on an altar wherever she wants to go. How many times is she ever going to come back to Cleveland? She's from here and she hardly ever comes back. Yes, kiss her beautiful butt for all it's worth when she is in town. Cities do all kinds of marketing campaigns to attract young people. Here's my campaign – "Come to Cleveland. Halle Berry is from here and we have even hotter chicks than her." Of course, it's not true, but who cares. Somehow, that gorgeous woman came from Cleveland. I say, "Let's take it and run with it for all it's worth."

I promised that I would always be honest and thorough in my storytelling. Let me preface my next statements by saying I am just attempting to repeat factual words that I have heard, and I am not attempting to make a racial commentary with these next comments. Let's be honest; there are some people who will not sleep with or date someone outside of their race.

Mayor David Bentkowski experiences love at first sight with actress Halle Berry.

I don't know if she is aware of it, but beautiful Halle Berry has come up in countless discussions about interracial dating. Here is a common conversation I have heard from white guys. The discussion usually starts with a white guy asking another white guy, "Would you ever be with a black girl?" There are a series of common answers that I have heard, ranging from "Yes, if it was Halle Berry" or "Are we talking Halle Berry or Star Jones?" Maybe it is because she has been voted *People's* Most Beautiful Person 100 times, but Halle Berry is the gold standard. I wonder if she knows that she is the person who is often used in these stupid comparisons and questions. There is not a straight guy in the world who wouldn't want to shag Halle Berry. There are others who receive the same treatment. Just a few paragraphs back, I used one of my favorite sayings, "I'm no Brad Pitt." Imagine you are so good looking that people use you as the standard! It must be very surreal.

My friend Laura Ambro orchestrated my Halle Berry meeting. Laura is sharp and gets it. She works for a company that promotes movies, and I have told her many times, "When the right premier comes to town, the City of Seven Hills is yours." We have a gorgeous swimming pool in Seven Hills and the next time there is a water-related movie like *Finding Nemo* or *Jaws* I want to have a dive-in-movie premier where the movie is shown on the giant wall while everyone is swimming in the water. Show us the money, Hollywood. I will even partially drain the zero-depth entry part of the pool to paint a red-carpet on it. Cool, right? Laura always hooked me up with good credentials. For Halle Berry I was a "reporter" on the line with a video camera asking Halle Berry a question. One thing I know is that celebrities love to talk about their charity work. By all accounts, Halle Berry does a lot of charity work so my question was simple, "Tell me about your favorite charitable causes?" There were about 100 reporters and cameras waiting to talk to her, and Halle Berry spent the longest time with me. She was with me for so long because I asked the right question. It was like throwing a hitter a high fastball. I could see her gorgeous eyes light up, and she was excited to talk about something of interest to her. She touched on about four of her causes as fast as she could. Truth be told, I didn't hear a word she said because all I could do was stare at her. In my defense, it was Halle Berry. Let me answer your question for you. Yes, she is that beautiful. In fact, she is even more beautiful in person. The woman does not have a pore on her face. I could stare at her face for an hour and I would not find a speck, or a dot, or a wrinkle, or anything else other than flawless skin. In person, her face looks like a perfect airbrushed magazine cover. What does this have to do with anything? Nothing, but I just like remembering that I met Halle Berry. Did you know that Halle Berry had a baby with white male model Gabrielle Aubry? I wonder if he was one of those guys who said, "Yeah, I'd be with a black chick." Imagine the children of Halle Berry and Gabrielle Aubry. Talk about hitting the gene lottery. There is some serious pressure on their kid to be good looking. It's like Andres Agassi and Steffi Graf's kid. I'm pretty sure that kid is going to make the tennis team.

Giovanni Ribisi was also in *Perfect Stranger* with Halle Berry, and he was gracious with his time as well at the Cinemark premier. It was fun to meet a young actor like him because no one knows what will happen in his career. The guy can act; maybe in 20 years, he will be like Mr. Costner and I will have my picture with him from his early days. He also talked about his charity efforts and seemed very social. I can imagine being a young handsome movie star. Brothers and sisters, that would be some fun time. We should all get together and try and make that happen for me because I promise I would tell every detail of every story. I hope you are entertained with my little proclamation dog and pony show. But wow, give me that type of fame and access and I'll make some stories happen that people wouldn't believe.

Yes, movie stars are just people and that is why they are in play and reachable if someone is smart and genuine. They have to hang out with someone, so why not me? I don't seek to use them; rather, I seek to be different

Mayor David Bentkowski with actor Giovanni Ribisi.

from everyone else: honest, and sincere with them. Sure, I help them if I can while they are in my town, but if I am a down-to-earth person that they can hang with instead of some phony Hollywood type, they welcome my company.

They have to network, promote and film their movies somewhere. Why not try and bring them to Seven Hills or Cleveland? We have thousands of great people in Seven Hills. They would be movie extras for free. My grannies would make pierogies and stuffed cabbage for the film crews. Whatever, we would love to have everyone and share our special place. Mayor Jackson, I know this isn't your thing; just give me a call and I'll make it happen and I'll have a blast doing it.

Cleveland Rocks and Laughs and Loses in Sports

Don't get me wrong, when I am critical about Cleveland or its leaders, it is because I love Cleveland and want it to reach its potential. Even though I have been to a million different places, it just dawned on me that other than my three years at the University of Toledo, I have lived my entire live in Greater Cleveland. If you were from Cleveland and I was proving my "street credibility" to you, I could give you an impressive list of points that would confirm that I am a "son" of the city. For example, I was here during John Elway's 98-yard scoring drive beating the Browns, freezing my tail off in the Dawg Pound with my big brother, Mark. I hate John Elway. I hate Art Modell, and I am glad Gary Bauer of The Basement bought Modell's stadium toilet and made a mockery out of him in his bar in the 1990s. I was even happier that Gary gave me a VIP pass for The Basement in its heyday, and I never had to wait in line. Yep, that was me dancing on the washing machine to New Order.

My mom would take me to get chocolate malts in the lower level of Higbee's or the May Company. I could never remember which was which. I just remember my mom could walk around the same clothes rack hundreds of times and still act like it was new to her. As Chris Rock would say, Parmatown Mall was the mall where white people used to shop. I also used to listen to the *Buzzard Morning Zoo* on WMMS 100.7 with Jeff and Flash and would get up to hear the "Token Joke of the Morning." I loved the movie *Major League* and would watch it on Opening Day religiously until the Cleveland Indians were a contender. Judging by their recent performance, it might be time to dust it off again.

I remember those dumb zoo keys that I could never get to work at the Cleveland Metroparks Zoo. Incidentally, my "uncle" Al Lewandowski was the head veterinarian at the zoo when I was in high school. His wife, Karen, is my Godmother. For years, I wanted to take this hot girl Kim Brooks on a date. Finally, she agreed to go with me because I promised her that "Uncle Al" would hook us up with a special tour. I had no idea what this meant. I told Kim that we could play with monkeys and get some kind of VIP treatment. Well, we got a special tour, but I forgot that Uncle Al was sort of a nerd. I say that with love, but he was a brilliant science guy. His idea of a special tour was the educational tour. My dreams of petting Kim while she petted a polar bear quickly faded when we started our tour. To a scientist like Uncle Al, it was fascinating to see how the sick animals are nursed to health and to discuss their illnesses. To hot Kim Brooks, it made her sick to her stomach, and she wanted to leave in five minutes. Thanks, Uncle Al!

I would throw up 22-footers like World B. Free when I played hoops, and I had a Jerry Dybzinski Indian's jersey – the Dibber! I played softball and baseball at Tremont, Gordon Park, State Road Park, and currently at James Day Park. My great uncle was Chet O'Block, the owner of Pyramid Café, the softball team that was World Champions in the 1970s, winning it all against those stacked southern teams. My grandfather on my mom's side, Grandpa Joe, was a Cleveland baseball sandlot legend and worked for Fisher Foods, and my grandmother Mollie worked at May Company, Regency Tire and the Jesuit Retreat House. I never met my Grandpa Joe, but from pictures he was a handsome guy who could easily handle anyone. All he cared about in life was my grandmother, my mom and her sister Geri. Grandpa Joe's brothers, Johnny and Pete, both had a rich baseball history. Johnny played professional baseball – second base – and Pete was a long-time scout for the Philadelphia Phillies. My dad's dad, also named Joe, worked at Ford.

My dad worked at J&L Steel and LTV Steel while my mom worked for 45 years on Public Square at Key Bank. My brother Mark is a union guy at the same steel mill where my dad worked. My brother Bryan started as one of Cleveland's most famous models, working for the agency of David & Lee. He was in the paper almost every day, and when I would go to the drugstore, he was the six-foot cardboard cutout for Hallmark cards. He is a successful pharmaceutical representative. My sister worked for a long time at "Cleveland's Own" Fox-8 television station as a Director.

As for me, one of my first jobs was working as a waiter at Denny's on Rockside Road. In what I would deem a cool piece of trivia, I was hired to replace Cleveland's favorite son, Drew Carey. Can't you picture Drew working at Denny's? It had to be awesome. It was the summer of my senior year between high school and college. Drew had just left to do comedy tours, and I needed to raise money for college. I would work at Denny's from 10 p.m. to 6:00 a.m. and wait on all the drunks who stopped off at the I-77/Rockside exit to sober up before driving home. After my shift at Denny's, I would go to work at LTV Steel from 6:30 a.m. to 2:30 p.m. These were two of the worst jobs of my life and it is probably because of them that I did well in college, graduating from Toledo in only three years while paying my own way.

Keep in mind this was also my senior summer before college. I was going to graduation parties and having a fun summer no matter my lack of sleep. I can't even begin to explain how tired I was. At Denny's, I was a waiter and also a host. One time I was working as a host and I was so tired, I fell asleep standing at the podium with a lobby full of people. During bar rush, there would be over an hour wait and the lobby was filled with drunks. When I woke up, everyone started clapping and cheering for me. I remember walking people to a table and customers looking at me and laughing. I'm sure I looked funny. It was not funny when drunks threw food at me. I was 18 years old and trying to pay for college. Really, they had some good reason to hit me on the side of my face with scrambled eggs? In case you were wondering, yes, if you throw food at someone, he will remember your face and do stuff to your food the next time you come to the restaurant, so touché! Denny's is a weird place at 3:00 a.m. There are the drunks, the newspaper guys starting their day, and yes, the occasional "lady of the evening." There was this gross lady who would come in every week and order one piece of toast and hot tea AFTER the act. Yuck, the tiny hairs on my neck stand up just thinking about it. If she ever ordered eggs, I was going to say, "Let me guess, you want your eggs unfertilized." I love that joke!

While working at Denny's that summer, there was a group of Cleveland Indians players who would come in after a late night of partying. Some of them lived in the neighboring hotels for the summer and would grab some grub, often with some female companionship, before heading home. Attention women: stop sleeping with professional athletes!!!! Who would think that Denny's would provide me with a life-lesson and early training for this book and my celebrity encounters, but it did. There was a relief pitcher named Kevin Wickander. Like most teenage boys, I knew every single player on the Indians, and like *Rain Man* I could tell you their statistics, where they went to college, and a ton of other useless stuff. We're boys, it's what we do. Kevin Wickander walked in one night with about an hour wait. He walked up in front of everyone and made a huge scene because he played for the Indians and he was not waiting. I said, "I'm sorry, sir, you are going to have to wait like everybody else." He was not amused. He waited about 20 minutes and came back to me and said, "Kid, I'll give you 100 bucks, just seat me already." If you are 18 and hosting at Denny's, 100 bucks is a night's wages. But, again, Vic and Barbara Bentkowski would be proud because I politely declined. Finally, after an hour, it was his time to sit and eat. Even though I was glad that I stuck to my guns, I was only 18 and nervous that he might get me into trouble. Other than when I was sleeping at the podium from exhaustion, I was normally a good worker. Even though I like to work smart and not hard, when there is work to be done, no one steps it up harder than I do. That night, we were slammed and I remember helping out all of the waitresses even though I was hosting. I was bussing tables, pouring coffee, bringing out food. I was all over the restaurant helping my co-workers give better service and make more tips. I remember glancing over at Kevin's table a couple of times, and it felt like he was watching me. I was nervous that he was going to get me fired or something.

As the host, I was also in charge of the register and sure enough, I had to wait on him when he came to pay his bill. After an awkward few moments of silence, he said, "Sorry I was demanding before. I hope there are no hard feelings." At that moment, I had an epiphany. At that moment, I got it. It dawned on me that the best ways to have people help me is to be cool to them and treat them with respect. Hard feelings? Why would I have hard feelings? I love the Cleveland Indians. I love anyone who plays for the Cleveland Indians. I knew every stat of Kevin Wickander's. I just wanted to do the right thing because that is how I was raised, and I didn't want some scene in front of everyone else. We shook hands and laughed about it. He came in a few weeks later and didn't even come up to the podium to give his name because he was waiting for someone. The wait was about an hour again, and it looked like he was debating whether or not to stay. We finally made eye contact and I raised and shook my fingers as if to say how many. He flashed back two fingers. "Wick, party of two. Wick, party of two," I announced. The drunks in the lobby never thought twice about it, and Kevin ate his eggs, got his sleep, and picked up the win for the Indians the following day. I never saw him again, but right before I went away to college, there was a card for me from him at the counter. It had $100 in it and a note from Kevin, "Good luck in school, you'll do just fine."

If someone is from Cleveland, he loves Drew Carey; I met him a couple of times at The Basement, which was the coolest bar ever when I was in college. It had one of my city council campaign signs up behind the bar in 1995, thanks to my friend Sonda Wolfe. The Basement was in the Cleveland Flats; at one time, I would put The Flats up against any party location in the country. Shooters, Fagan's, The Basement, Jimmy's, Bar Cleveland, Have a Nice Day Café, The Smart Bar, The River's Edge; they were all great. I cannot tell you the fun I had in those places. As the funny Mike Polk recently sang, it now looks like a *Scooby Doo* ghost town. Drew was huge in Cleveland during this heyday for The Flats. What is not to love about Drew Carey? He is best friend material. When Drew would walk into The Basement, it wasn't like a famous television star was in the building. It was, "Holy Crap, it's Drew. Oh, my God, I love Drew. Let's go shake his hand." There would be a line of guys and girls waiting to give Drew some love. The guys would buy him a beer and shake his hand. The girls would give him hugs and kisses. If ever there were a guy to cheer for and be glad that he made it, Drew was the guy. It is hard to explain how much Clevelanders love Drew, but he could shoot 10 people and the prosecutor would probably have a tough time finding a Cleveland jury to convict him. "Those crazy people jumped in front of those bullets."

In addition to Denny's, my other bond with Drew was Hilarities Comedy Club, which is now part of Pickwick and Frolic. When people think of a comedy club, they usually think some dumpy hole in the wall. Hilarities 4th Street Theater is the most beautiful club in the country. It was an old Opera House and owner Nick Kostis created the most unique space. It has an awesome restaurant, martini bar, midnight lounge acts, modern bar and the best comics in the country. Hilarities is a must stop for any comedian. Of course, Drew was no stranger to the club. When I was 17 and in high school, Nick used to own an old Hilarities club with a guy named Paul Duffy. I was friends with his son, also named Paul, at Padua Franciscan High School. I always have liked to perform before an audience. I convinced Paul Jr. to trick his dad into letting me perform at amateur night. I was 17 and took the stage to a packed house. Normally, amateur night was lucky to have 30 people in attendance. Well, this night was some special event for a local charity. The room was sold out and people were standing in the aisles and in back. I didn't tell anyone I was doing the comedy segment because I had no idea how I would do, and I figured there was no way my parents would let me do it. Some of my friends told my parents what I was up to, and when I came out on stage, I looked in the front row and there was my mother, my father, my sister, and my sweet grandmother. Now the bad news – my set was one of the dirtiest sets I could ever imagine a 17-year-old doing. I totally stole jokes from some comedians I had seen on HBO. I stole the joke about how one time I was fooling around on a couch with a girl and she said, "We can't do this, I'm going to the gynecologist tomorrow and I never like to do it before I see him." In reply, I said, "You're not going to the dentist, too, are you?" I also had a bunch of my own dirty jokes and stories. Between the funny jokes I stole and my own decent material, I killed the place. I looked so young and was so innocent that it just made the dirty jokes more effective. When I saw my parents and grandmother, I said, "Here goes nothing" and I did the entire dirty set. My grandmother had the greatest sense of humor and as soon as I got going, she was crying because she was laughing so hard. It gave me energy and I gave the comedy set of my life. Yes, my parents grounded me for weeks for my swear words and sneaking into a bar at 17, but they also said I was amazing and said I could pursue that field if I wanted because I had "it." College and law school prevailed, but who knows, I could have been the next Drew Carey.

Nick Kostis has become a dear friend over the years, and I can honestly say "I love that guy." He is just awesome, gracious, and a larger-than-life personality. As mayor, I called him on a whim, and he remembered me as the 17-year-old kid who snuck into his club. I asked him if I could interview the comedians every week for my local cable access show. He said, "Sure,

Mayor David Bentkowski with comedian Hal Sparks.

why not?" Thanks to Nick and John Lorince, I interviewed every comedian who came into Hilarities for a year. To name a few, I met Lou Ramey, Jon Fish, Hal Sparks, John Campanera, and my all-time favorite, Greg Fitzsimmons.

Greg is probably the funniest person I have ever met in my life. You might know him as an Emmy Award-winning writer for *The Ellen DeGeneres Show.* You might know him as a friend of *The Howard Stern Show* and his own hilarious show on satellite radio. You might also know him from VH1-s *Best Week Ever* shows. You might also know him as the frequent host of the Adult Video Awards Show in Las Vegas. Yep, believe it or not, there is an awards show for the adult film industry. "Mom, Dad, big news, I won the award for best *$&%bang." I can almost hear that girl's parents committing suicide. I wonder if any porn parent has ever put that in a Christmas letter.

I met Greg Fitzsimmons the day after I met Omarosa in what had to be fate. That afternoon, we all went to the funniest lunch hour of my life. I am nowhere near as funny as Greg Fitzsimmons, but I held my own, and I think he found me amusing. Whenever he comes to town, I try to help him out or at least visit him and most importantly, catch his show. For one show, I was backstage with Greg and John Lorince. Nick came in and said, "Greg, Smith Barney has 100 people here tonight. It is a corporate outing and they paid a ton of money. Do not do any vulgar jokes or curse a lot. And whatever you do, do not make fun of anyone in the audience." Ten seconds after Greg took the stage, he was making fun of the Smith Barney people. He did 45-minutes off the cuff, and it was the funniest 45-minutes I will ever hear in my life. Like a brilliant surgeon, he started interviewing and analyzing every one

Mayor David Bentkowski with Cleveland reggae legend Carlos Jones.

of the Smith Barney people in attendance. He worked his way to the top boss and made fun of him for about 15 minutes. Everyone in the room, including the big boss, was crying and laughing hysterically. I remember standing outside the exits as these people in suits left, and I heard the boss say, "My God, that was the most fun I have ever had. We are coming back next year."

Another time, Greg had some time to kill. We went to a Cleveland Indians game during the day. My friend Ron Tryczinski, owner of the Original Mattress Factory and fellow Pollack, hooked me up with seats right behind home plate. The entire game, Greg was just talking out loud making jokes and funny observations. The entire section was laughing and listening to him. No one was even paying attention to the game. Greg would just see something or someone and start making jokes, and the people were rolling. He is easily the funniest stand-up comic I have ever seen.

I never thought about these little perks, but even having the chance to see the best comics in the world is something I can do in Cleveland versus some other small city. In addition to great comics, Cleveland is a great place for music. Michael Hampton of P-Funk is from Cleveland, but there are many more on the list. On any given weekend in Cleveland, I can go check out dozens of awesome bands. One of my all-time favorites is reggae legend Carlos Jones and the PLUS (Peace, Love, Unity, Syndicate) Band. I grew up going to see Carlos front First Light and the I-Tals. I could listen to reggae all the time. Other great Cleveland bands and artists include The Waterband, who once performed their hit single "For You" in honor of my mother on the show *Around Town*. Check out Rachel Roberts, Peter Niro, the Hol-

Mayor David Bentkowski with rock icon Deborah Harry of Blondie.

lywood Shuffle with Patrick and Brittany Bittel, the Michael Stanley Band, trumpet protégé Dominick Farinacci, Alexis Antes, Odd Girl Out, Sax-O-Tromba, Third Wish, and the Spazmatics. There are also Polka greats such as Majestic Sound. That's right, you heard me, Polka greats! Cleveland is worthy because every major tour stops in the city. It is the Rock and Roll Capital of the World, after all.

One of my favorite meet and greets was Debbie Harry of Blondie. In my mind, she is in the Top 3 of the most influential women in music history. It's kind of funny, but she has a slight resemblance to my mother – both back in the 1970s and today. I tried to find out her ethnicity, but she looks like she might be Polish or Hungarian or something. She has beautiful light skin and a round face. I have seen Debbie Harry and Blondie several times in concert, but seeing her perform a solo show and meeting her was quite a thrill. Her show was a couple of years ago the night before Thanksgiving. Why Debbie Harry is at the Agora the night before Thanksgiving is beyond me, but I'm glad she was. What struck me as interesting is that the crowd was packed with young kids. She was showing off some of her new solo material and these kids were singing every word to every song. It made me happy for her. She is such a legend; it was fun to see her in her 60s receiving this kind of love and affection from a new generation. She kindly accepted her proclamation and graciously posed for several pictures. I was a little nervous about her doing something with the proclamation because let's not forget, she is a punk queen. I once saw a guy give her a dozen roses at a concert and one by one she bit the buds off and spit them at the guy. It was awesome and the guy loved it because that is exactly what he would expect Debbie Harry to do.

Oh, the stories she must have. Can you imagine hanging with her in the 1970s at Studio 54 or CBGBs in New York? It had to be the ultimate party. I have loved her music for many, many years. Her new stuff is great and had success on dance charts. She's hugely popular like Madonna. There is a whole dance and subculture that still worships her. If you go to dance clubs in New York, they are playing Debbie Harry's old and new stuff. I just think the world of her and I am grateful that I met her. Some younger people might not know her legacy, but since I have met her, when I rattle off the names of people I have met, a lot of people will stop me and say things like, "Oh my God, you met Debbie Harry, that's awesome." For those in the know, they realize just what a historic musical icon she is. I would love to set up a lunch with Mom, Debbie Harry and me. That would be fun.

Sports are another great thing to enjoy in Cleveland. Well, we enjoy until our team eventually loses and breaks our hearts. I have probably met over 100 local athletes, and most have been cool. Cleveland Browns Quarterback Brady Quinn was social and was good friends with my good friend and Casket Store teammate Doug Phillips. I once met some girl at jury duty who claimed she was dating Brady Quinn. She made a big production at jury duty that she might have to miss a day because she was going to see her boyfriend Brady play in the Browns Monday Night game in Buffalo. My friend, Doug, who talks to Brady on occasion, said Brady was like, "Are you kidding me? I have been dating the same girl forever. I'm not flying some girl out to Buffalo."

It reminded me of one of my favorite celebrity stories about me. I am always fascinated why people exaggerate a story or tell a lie to look good. One time, I was at the Blind Pig in Cleveland with my friend and former Casket Store teammate Jeff Phillips. Jeff is my usual wing-man when I am single. We are both non-aggressive and just sort of hang out together in bars because we are not sleazy guys trying to sleep with every girl in the bar. We just go out to leave work stress for awhile; if we meet and talk to cute girls, that is a bonus.

I had gone to the bathroom and upon my return Jeff smoothly was talking to two beautiful girls. I joined the conversation and one girl was complain-

Mayor David Bentkowski with quarterback Brady Quinn of Notre Dame and the Cleveland Browns.

ing how she got a ticket in, of all places, Seven Hills. Jokingly, I said, "Oh, maybe I can help you with that ticket."

She said, "Oh, I don't need your help. I know the mayor."

I said, "Really, you know the mayor? Wow, how do you know him?"

She said, "Oh, we party together all the time. You know, he's that young guy. I've been friends with him for years." I looked over at Jeff, and he was about to wet his pants he was laughing so hard. I said to the girl, "That's funny, I heard the mayor is pretty straight-laced. I heard he's not much of a partier because he works all the time."

She said, "Oh, no, he's a total partier. He gets crazy. He's also my lawyer. If I ever get in trouble, he'll help me out." You get the idea, I let her talk for about five minutes more, and then it was time to go. As I was leaving, I handed her one of my "mayor" cards and said, "Let me know how that ticket works out for you." God gives us little gifts in life to enjoy. Trust me, folks - the look on her face when she read the card was a gift I'll never forget.

It brings me back to my question of, "Why would someone lie about something stupid?" Why would a girl say she was dating Brady Quinn when she was not? Why would a hot girl say she knew me – when she didn't – and she didn't even know she was talking to me? If you are going to say you know a mayor, heck, say you know Rudy Giuliani, not little David Bentkowski.

Once, Omarosa came to town to help Cleveland Brown Rueben Droughns launch his charity, and we worked selling raffle tickets at his tailgate party. When it was game time, Omarosa and I had the chance to sit in either Gary Baxter's loge or Rueben Droughns' loge. This would prove to be a great business lesson. I met both of them previously, and they were both great guys.

What was amazing to me was to see how differently the people around them acted. In Gary Baxter's loge, there were only five people counting me. There was Omarosa, Gary's mother, a big scary looking guy who could have been an agent or bodyguard, and Michelle Williams of Destiny's Child, Gary's girlfriend at the time. When I showed up in the loge, everyone was very into the game, and I felt out of place. While Omarosa stayed behind, I went to Rueben's loge. Rueben's loge was like a P-Funk party. The loge was supposed to seat about 10. I would guess that between 20 and 30 people were coming and going in the room. Rueben had cousins, and friends, agents, and all kinds of people in there who probably didn't even have a ticket. One guy would leave with three tickets and bring back three people. What I remember most was when the dessert cart came. The dessert cart was the devil. Seriously, it was filled with the most amazing desserts I ever saw in my life. Problem was they were about $10 each. The cart was parked outside Rueben's loge for what seemed like an hour. There was this huge line of people getting desserts from the cart. There were people from other loges getting into line and everything was getting billed to Rueben. After watching this for a few minutes, I felt bad for him and shut it down. I said to the attendant, "What are you doing giving all these people desserts. They are not even in this loge. Stop billing all this to Rueben." In a flash, the dessert crowd dissolved.

The lesson was that people will steal any chance they can. Rueben was on the field getting tackled by a 300-pound lineman and his "peeps" were in his loge being careless with his money. All I could think of was MC Hammer going broke despite making $30 million that year. He tried to help all his friends and they all took advantage of him. I'm hoping Rueben and some of these other guys keep some of their money because sooner or later, the gravy train stops and the millions aren't rolling into their pockets. I have a bad feeling that once the money is gone, so are the friends. Rueben was a good guy and I hope that doesn't happen to him. Gary Baxter did it right. It was people he could trust, and my guess is he'll keep his money for a long time.

Other local favorites I met include Braylon Edwards of the Browns, who stepped up and donated $1 million to the Cleveland Schools. Now that is what I am talking about as far as charity. Donating that kind of loot is a real gesture of concern, not some bogus photo opportunity where a player shows up and reads to the kids. Big deal, they can read. Now show us the money!

If I could magically trade places with someone, I would probably pick Cleveland Indians outfielder Grady Sizemore. The guy is young, good looking, has a $25 million contract, was an All-Star and Gold Glove winner, and by most accounts, is a shy guy who likes to hang out with family and friends. I've met him several times, and to some he may come off as smug, but apparently he is just quiet if he doesn't know you.

Growing up, one of my favorite meetings was Cleveland Browns quarterback Bernie Kosar. He is like Drew Carey in that Clevelanders are going to love him forever. Those were magical games watching Bernie and the Browns from the Dawg Pound and I love listening to Bernie do current Browns television analysis because he knows so much about football. Bernie is like legendary Chicago Cubs announcer, Harry Caray. He says whatever he feels. During a recent Browns game, Bernie described the Browns as being "awful" and said to the television audience, "God bless you if you are still watching this."

I have only been on for a few months, but Facebook has proven to be fun. I am "friends" with Browns alumnae Top Dawg Hanford Dixon, running back Kevin Mack, running back Herman Fontenot, Ohio State basketball player Brad Sellers, NFL legends Keith Byars and Rod Woodson, and Ohio State great and two-time Heisman Trophy Winner, the one, the only, Archie Griffin.

I love THE Ohio State Buckeyes and have met players by helping a great charity called Cornerstone of Hope. Mark and Christi Tripodi woke up one Mother's Day with their three-year-old son, Bobby, sick. Hours later, Bobby passed away. I can't imagine what a nightmare this would be for any couple. These

Mayor David Bentkowski and NFL receiver Braylon Edwards discuss his $1 million donation to the Cleveland Public Schools.

two amazing people learned first-hand that there was no bereavement center for people who experience this kind of loss. As if hand-picked by God, they dedicated their lives to raising money and building the Cornerstone of Hope. Thanks to their efforts and a lot of others, there is this amazing place in Independence, Ohio, right next to Seven Hills, where people can get help when they need it most. Their beautiful little boy loved Superman so they use a picture of him in a Superman costume; I want to cry every time I look at it. God bless them and all they have done for the world. I am truly humbled just to know them. Please visit them at www.cornerstoneofhope. org and help their cause. Every year at their big banquet, some Buckeyes that live in the area attend for everyone to meet. I have enjoyed being a casino dealer for fun games with fake money. I hold court every year with a bunch of players I know. I make them laugh, and they get a kick out of the funny mayor. One year, a girlfriend was sitting next to me while I dealt, and one of the players came to the table and started flirting with her. The other players started laughing and said, "Dude, that's the mayor's girl." I chimed in, "You better check yo-self before you wrickity wrickity wreck yo-self!" The other players started teasing him and told him that he would get pulled over on his way home. Over the years I have befriended some of the players and they have been fun contacts. Every now and then I'll send them a funny text or joke about beating Michigan. Rob Rose and Thaddeus Gibson are two of my favorites. Over the years Alex Gonzalez, Terrelle Pryor, Robert Smith, Ted Ginn and, most of all, Coach John Cooper have donated their time and money to the Cornerstone of Hope.

Current Coach Jim Tressel is another person who walks on water in Ohio. The guy beats Michigan. Enough said! In addition, he is a throwback to an old-school coach who teaches right from wrong. I have been at fundraisers where Coach Tressel was the keynote speaker. He will drive almost three hours from Columbus to Cleveland, give his free talk to help the charity, and hop back in his car to drive three hours home so he can be at work in the morning. It is not an act. It is not for publicity. He is Coach Jim Tressel, and if ever you wanted to cheer for someone - cheer for him because he is a lesson in how we should all act.

There you have it, stories from Cleveland, Ohio. Great food. Great music. Great sports. Great art. Great people. Great neighborhoods. Great Lake. But more than anything else, it is home. Go Browns!

Mayor David Bentkowski and NFL star Ted Ginn.

Mayor David Bentkowski and Ohio State quarterback Terrelle Pryor.

Mayor David Bentkowski with Ohio State football coach, Jim Tressel.

Mayor David Bentkowski loves his Ohio State Buckeyes!

Bobby Tripodi continues to inspire people's lives and you can help his memory and the mission of the Cornerstone of Hope by donating. Visit www.cornerstoneofhope.org. Superman would be proud!

Justin Timberlake and David Bentkowski: "Dance, white boys, dance!"

I am not a fan of stereotypes because they are seldom accurate. Remember the LL Cool J chapter? I also learned this while playing in my recreational basketball league. My friend Tim secured three black guys to play hoops with us. He might as well have secured Steve Erkel, Emmanuel Lewis and Gary Coleman because these were the three worst basketball players I have ever seen. Really, Tim, out of all the black guys in the world who are awesome at basketball, these were the three you brought us? Tiger Woods is the greatest golfer in the world and Eminem is the greatest rapper in the world. Good-bye stereotypes, hello judging individuals on merit.

By the way, can black people stop making sport movies about overcoming some team barrier created by whites? They are running out of sports to profile. A movie about Jackie Robinson breaking the color barrier in baseball is great. I'm talking about the Denzel Washington-type movies where the black swim team "overcomes" and wins a swim meet. Or the black chess team takes on Harvard. The plot line is tired. We get it. Black people are great. I mean really, what's next? I can hear that guy with the serious announcer voice saying in a preview, "They said he couldn't do it. They said he was crazy. But John wanted to be the first African-American to win the polka contest." Movies with this "us versus them" mentality hurt racial harmony.

In 2008 a whole lot of white people helped make Barack Obama the first black President. Blacks account for about 12% of the population, and President Obama whooped a truly great American, John McCain. Senator John McCain was a war hero. He was tortured in a Vietnam prison for many years and still acted with honor and never sold out this great country. As if that weren't enough, he came back and served his country for decades more in the Senate. No offense to President Obama, but if ever a guy paid his dues and deserved to be President, it was McCain. Tens of millions of white people voted for President Obama so everyone please quit playing the race card. We all know everyone from every race and ethnic origin can accomplish anything they want in life so let go of the crutch and everyone contribute to a better America. I'm tired of hearing about everyone's special interest or alleged burdens. I want to hear how everyone wants to help our country.

Another popular stereotype is that white guys can't sing and dance. Ladies and gentleman of the jury, I would like to offer Mr. Justin Timberlake as Exhibit A to counter that bogus claim. Make no mistake about it, my all-time favorite encounter and the guy who deserves credit for being cooler and classier than anyone else is Justin Timberlake.

It shouldn't have surprised me because Justin is from Memphis, Tennessee, and if you have ever spent time in Tennessee, you would know the people there couldn't be nicer. Yes, people from Ohio are nice, but some Southerners are over-the-top nice. Justin Timberlake deserves every great thing that happens to him. For starters, he could not be more talented. I was blown away by his talent during his concert.

Pop culture is funny. There is this script where guys will knock a guy like Justin because they are worried others will tease them if they admit they like him. In high schools and colleges across the country, it is almost a reflex for guys to make fun of boy bands and call them "gay." Don't forget, the guy who is a silly homophobe and feels the need to hate on others is usually the guy who wants some hairy guy named Bruce to tie him to a bed post. It is assumed young guys will make fun of groups like Hanson, the Backstreet Boys and Justin's old group, N'SYNC. Every now and then, someone is so talented he can rise above that cliché ridicule and emerge. Justin is that guy.

I am secure enough to say, "Absolutely, Justin Timberlake is great." The guy can sing, dance, entertain; he can do it all. In addition, from a guy's guy perspective, he is an avid golfer, is funny and pokes fun at himself with great *Saturday Night Live* skits, and allegedly hooked up with Brittany Spears, Cameron Diaz, Scarlett Johannson, Alyssa Milano and Jessica Biel. I don't know if his "girl" list is true, but if it is, "Good for you, brother!" He has conducted himself in such a way that even if some "Average Joe" in Peoria wants to hate him because of his success, he can't because the guy is a good guy.

I'm proud of him. There is much reverse racism in the world and a growing, disgusting sentiment that making fun of white guys is the only safe politically correct play anymore. It is refreshing to have a young white kid receive recognition and respect in pop culture.

Much like Gwen Stefani, Justin and his people are on top of everything. Most of the people affiliated with his tour are related to him, are friends of his, or are from his home in Tennessee. It is striking to see how much the people who work for him appear to truly love him and that only reaffirms my belief that he must be a class act who treats people well. If he were a jerk, my guess is I could pick up on it from the spirit of those around him.

I called to meet him on short notice. Within minutes, his people were making it happen, and they were precise and thorough. At the meet and greet Justin had some woman greet everyone and spend 15 minutes talking about Justin and his tour. I want to say she was a relative or long-time family friend but I can't remember for sure. This was a unique, classy touch. Her talk was very interesting and she painted a picture for me. She talked about the enterprise of the tour such as how many workers and busses there were and talked about life on the road. She talked about the stage and the concert vision and how the ideas came together (virtually every aspect is from the mind of Justin). She talked about everything a nerd like me would want to know. Again, she talked with such fond affection for Justin it was palpable. Instead of just wanting to get it over with, she was going out of her way to make sure everyone walked away with the greatest encounter of their lives.

I had a separate meeting with Justin and throughout the entire process every single person on his team was friendly, courteous and professional. I was standing in the hallway waiting a couple minutes for the meet and greet and the security guard came out and said, "Mayor, I'm sorry, we are running a couple of minutes late. Is that okay? Can we help you with any arrangements?" I'm laughing in my head thinking, "Oh, I'm sure my limo motorcade can wait." Seriously, dude, where did I have to go? I can wait an hour to meet Justin. They were doing me the favor.

Finally, I met Justin and he was great. He is a guy I would have been friends with in high school. He is funny, upbeat, talkative and appreciative. He took a ton of pictures with my group and was extremely accommodating. He even gave me a shout out during the concert.

Mayor David Bentkowski and singer Justin Timberlake.

I love when good things happen to good people. Whenever I hear someone knock someone like Justin, I call him on it and point out that he shouldn't be jealous; he should try and be more like him. Good people treat others well. Eventually good actions will trump negative gossip. I have even seen it in politics. In politics, people I beat in an election or who oppose me will say mean things about me or try and turn others against me. The best way to counter that is just work hard, be a good person, and stay focused on a positive agenda.

Over time, when I keep getting good things done for the community, people will become my defenders. I have heard multiple stories similar to this in my life. Someone with an agenda might be at a little league game and start talking smack about me. Time and time again, people I don't even know will speak up and say, "'You know, you should shut your mouth because he is the best mayor we have ever had, and I am getting sick of you making up lies about him behind his back." Think about it, why would you want to be on the side of the guy talking about people, being negative, and acting scurrilous? No, the correct answer is you want to be friends with the guy who is a winner and just does his thing and doesn't try to build himself up by tearing down others. What's that famous quote: "Great people talk about ideas. Average people talk about things. Small people talk about other people." I have only talked about one person while being mayor and it was a candidate who should not have been elected; I was duty bound to share what I knew. Yes, I realize that this is a book about other people, but by now you should know that this is not a mean-spirited book and I cast a favorable light on virtually everyone who deserves it.

One thing that is difficult for me to shine a favorable light on is my dancing career. Yes, I am ashamed to admit that I can dance. I don't necessarily like it, I just can do it. Dancing is not something I usually seek to do unless I have a purpose. I would dance in the basement of Frankie's in Toledo to New Order, the Cure and Depeche Mode because that is what Jennifer wanted to do on our dates in college. Jen was this beautiful little Polish girl from Toledo, and yep, when I was 19, she made a man out of me for my first time. She still sends me a Christmas card every year, nearly 20 years later. I sent her a Facebook message to confirm she was cool with me revealing this fact, and she laughed at my foolishness and said yes. If ever I were going to write a perfect first-time, Jen would be the girl. She was so hot and sweet and thought my awkwardness was adorable. I was Michael Cera in *Juno* before he was even born. We loved the same music, the same movies, everything. Of course, I was a total dork and her act of charity will always be cherished and remembered by me. As if that isn't enough of a pressure moment for a guy in life, I had this piece of junk couch that was only part of the sectional. It only had one side with an arm rest; I clearly remember the pillows sliding off the other side of the couch during our fun. They don't call me Mr. Romantic for nothing. That poor girl was pretty much on a spring frame with her head jammed in the corner by the time it was over. I hope to God I don't have daughters some day. I promise if I ever have a son, I am going to make sure he has a sturdy bed and couch when he goes off to college.

Another funny Frankie's story: I had a roommate in college who was a big, strong guy who liked country music. We were great friends and shared our backgrounds with each other. He would take me to country bars, and I would take him to progressive places like Frankie's. The lower level of Frankie's was where the dancing took place and it was virtually pitch black down there except for some strobe or dance lights. I was looking over at my roommate, and he was crying, he was laughing so hard. He could barely tell me the story. Apparently, he thought he was standing against a wall. In reality, his back and butt were up against some girl who was just standing close to him. She thought he was trying to flirt with her by standing there, so she didn't move. Well, she eventually moved because thinking she was the wall, my friend farted on her. The girl said, "Uh, that's my leg" and walked away probably to go vomit. Oh, that was funny. Can you imagine? I can still remember the tears coming down his face as he was telling that story.

When I came back to Cleveland, I used to dance at The Basement in The Flats. This was THE place to go and I may not have been MC Hammer, but I realized very early on that girls liked to dance – so I liked to dance. For you young guys who don't get it yet, no girl wants to talk to you if you are a wallflower with a dip cup looking to fight everyone. Dance floors are so crowded, even if you just stand there and bounce a little it will be good enough to get you closer to the action. (No need to thank me, just send a campaign donation and your wedding picture).

After being in long-term relationships for awhile, I hadn't danced in years until one day I received a phone call from Channel 5 WEWS/ABC reporter Alicia Scicolone. When Alicia first arrived in Cleveland, she was new and naïve and I asked her to emcee the Miss Seven Hills Pageant. She said yes, not knowing how much work it was. I was forever grateful and told her I would return the favor. Little did I know what that offer would cost me. Alicia called up and said "Hey, remember that favor you owe me? We are doing a Cleveland version of *Dancing with the Stars* with local celebrities. Will you do it for me?" I remember that she called early in the morning, probably hoping I would be half-awake as I made this ill-advised commitment. You know what happened next: I said, yes, not knowing the evil genie I was letting out of the bottle.

When I say I can dance, I mean I can do a couple moves; I have rhythm, and in a dark club with strobe lights, I can be decent enough not to embarrass myself. As I quickly learned, ball room dancing was a whole other beast.

The local celebrities were teamed up with professional dancers from studios in Cleveland. My partner was the beautiful and talented Rebecca Sweet of Viva Dance in Strongsville, Ohio. Rebecca does not mess around. She was all business and our partnership was brilliant and explosive at the same time. Deep down, I hate dancing. She loves dancing. Deep down, I don't like physical activity. She loves it. I am the type of guy who just likes to "wing" things and get the gist of it. Rebecca was a crazy perfectionist who wanted to focus on every little detail such as my arm positioning and the spacing of my steps. We could not be more opposite personalities, and it was amazing we didn't kill each other. Five minutes into our first practice, we were like an old married couple arguing and fighting.

There were 12 couples initially and we would all practice together. We had three hours each week to learn a new dance and then after the three hours, crews would film everyone twice for the actual television broadcast. One shot was from far away and one shot was close. This was very stressful because I had "zero" room for error. The contestants consisted of local radio and television personalities, Cleveland Browns players, and other community notables.

While practicing one day, Rebecca was watching one of our competitors, Doug the Hunky Firefighter. His real name was Doug Turner, and he was a popular firefighter in the community, but because he has muscles everywhere, all the women just referred to him as Doug the Hunky Firefighter. Why can't I get any love like that? No, I'm David the Noodle-Armed Choirboy.

Doug was doing all kinds of physical tricks with his partner, the beautiful dancer Samara McCullough. He was flipping her, bench pressing her, and spinning her on his finger like a Harlem Globetrotter. It was annoying.

Rebecca looked at me and said, "We need to do some of that!" Lady, are you out of your mind? Was there anything about my physical appearance that would lead her to believe I was capable of that? No!

Rebecca said, "Lie down on your back and spread your legs." I was thinking, "Finally, this dancing is going to go somewhere." She said, "Put your arms up in the air." And without any advance warning, she dove horizontally toward me. In her mind I think she had envisioned some romance novel where I caught

Mayor David Bentkowski and his professional dance partner, Rebecca Sweet of Viva Dance.

her in my arms and held her in the air as she posed, like a beautiful swan. In reality, my arms didn't consider trying to catch her for even a split second. In fact, out of reflex, my arms bailed like the French and retreated down to my sides. With her full force and weight, she landed perfectly horizontally on me. We've decided to keep the baby . . . Okay - that was the joke. But seriously, with a thunderous crash, she fell on top of me. She totally "popped" me in the "boys" with her leg. She hurt her hip. Everyone looked over at us and the two of us were rolling around on the ground in pain.

After that day, we dramatically reined in her expectations of what I would be capable of doing. I thought for sure I would lose in week one but something magical happened – voting. My grannies love me, and I love them. And if there is one thing to know about old people, they vote. Like an army, my grannies started voting like crazy for me. Week after week after week I was near the top of the vote totals, and I was easily gliding into the next round.

The good news was I hate to lose any election and the vote totals were good for my ego. The bad news was I really did hate ballroom dancing. Don't get me wrong, I have a new appreciation for it, but it was a nightmare. My butt hurt. My legs hurt. My "stuff" was constantly getting grazed by an errant leg kick. I was thinking of wearing an athletic cup to practice. I was hurting in places I didn't know I had. About halfway through the contest, I seriously was thinking about getting my friends to vote for other people so I could get off the show. It meant a lot to Rebecca to be able to show off her amazing talent every week so I sucked it up and persevered. More than any other instructor, she deserved praise because she did the most with the least. By the end of the competition, I was pretty good. I was flipping her and catching her by her neck. I was spinning her around over my head. I even learned how to do Michael Jackson's "moonwalk" and the Usher "slide."

We made it to the finals and ultimately came in second place to Laurie Hovater from 99.5 WGAR and her talented partner, Andy Slimak. Laurie was on the morning show for the local country station and guess what – people who listen to country music are good citizens, and they vote as much as old people so Laurie beat me fair and square. Laurie was one of the nicest people I ever met and we were all very happy for her that she won because she was a mom with kids, a great wife, and a hard-working professional. For her, this dancing was a great "escape" from her busy life. I'm glad I came in second because if I won, more of my buddies would still be making fun of me. I already have my softball team calling me "Twinkle-toes" when I'm batting because of it.

I lasted longer than any other guy celebrity and beat people who had a built-in edge. Every week, the television and radio people were constantly telling their viewers and listeners to vote for them. Every week, they had audiences of tens of thousands and somehow, I still lasted until the end. All I had was a white-haired army from Seven Hills going to the library trying to vote online for their favorite mayor.

It's not official, and I reserve the right to change my mind, but I'm going to pull a Brett Favre and announce my retirement from dancing for awhile. Between this contest and my performance in New Orleans during the Essence Festival, I can use a break. I will come out of retirement for two reasons: First, the next time Justin Timberlake is in town, I will join him on stage and be one-half of a dynamic duo of white boys who can dance, all in the name of crushing stereotypes. Or second, I will next dance with my lovely bride on our wedding day. Hmmm, I wouldn't bet the farm on either of these happening anytime soon.

Don't Hate Politicians, Love Them: President Bill Clinton, President George W. Bush, First Lady Laura Bush, Vice President Al Gore, Senator John Glenn, the Reverend Jesse Jackson, and many, many more.

When I would visit my grandmother, Mollie, growing up, her house was a shrine to President John F. Kennedy. She had photos of him on the wall, a table with news clippings about him under glass, and she even had a crocheted blanket of him. She loved her President. When I think of that, it makes me sad how disrespectful people have become toward our current leaders. I may not love, or even like, our recent leaders but everyone keeps forgetting that these people and the offices deserve and demand honor.

I don't care if it was Clinton, Bush or Obama, the minute they are elected, they are MY President and I want them to do well for MY country. Radical party activists on both the Republican and Democratic sides often lose sight of how their constant besmirching has a negative effect on our country, and I don't like it!

The President of the United States of America is the most powerful person in the world. I like that about our country. Our guy is the top dog! Although it is perfectly acceptable to disagree with policy and voice concern, the extent to which people mock, abuse, and attack our leaders has gotten out of hand.

Meeting celebrities can be difficult, but if you are willing to work hard, you can meet virtually any politician you want. There are always events where someone can meet a candidate or office holder. Yes, there are those expensive dinners that I would never attend. Instead, I just keep my eyes open for inexpensive events on the campaign trail, possibly volunteer, or show up at free rallies. Anyone can get a photo opportunity especially if they meet a candidate during a campaign.

The first President I met was Bill Clinton when he came to the University of Toledo. I could easily make a joke about Clinton coming to a college campus filled with hot coeds, but you already thought it in your head. Why bother? Presidential candidates always spend a ton of time visiting college campuses and until recently, I always thought it was a waste because those students hardly ever voted. Things have changed in the last couple of elections, but students do not vote as much as one would think. It may be because of absentee voting provisions, voter registration requirements, or a Theta Chi Fraternity keg party. Although I am a champion of young people getting involved in government, maybe it is a blessing that some of these people don't vote because their logic in choosing a candidate might not jive with my own.

I am starting to sound like an old person, but some 20-year-old voting for a President because the dude in the band Green Day told him to might not be what I want. If they do their research and have a clue, then fine, vote away. If they are an idiot, please don't ruin my country!

I always like to ask young people why they are voting for someone. It's not like I am usually rabid for either candidate. My views skip around depending on the issue. I just hate when an obvious idiot's vote is as important as mine. During the 2008 Presidential election, I was talking to this college-aged girl and she indicated she was voting for Barack Obama. I asked her why and she said "McCain looks old. He makes funny gestures with his arms." I asked her if she knew why McCain did that and she said "No, I don't know." I don't know what caused me to snap on her, probably patriotism, but I said, "He can't lift his arms all the way, you imbecile, because he was tortured in a Vietnam prison for years fighting for you!"

Look, vote for whomever you want. If you are pro-life or pro-choice, or pro-guns or against guns . . . those are issues that should impact your vote.

But, if you are so stupid that you are not voting for a true American hero because you think his arms look funny after he was injured on your behalf, then do us all a favor, and stay home and watch Jerry Springer on Election Day.

Surprisingly, nothing too exciting happened when I met President Clinton. He gave a great talk, it was crazy to see dozens of Secret Service guys on top of the University of Toledo buildings surrounding the student union/mall area with rifles, and this was when Clinton was just a candidate, right before he won. Love Clinton or not, you have to admit, *Saturday Night Live* made his presidency hilarious. There are two skits that stick out for me. First, I remember the funny line where the great Phil Hartman was playing Clinton, visiting a fast-food joint during a jog. Clinton eats a giant hamburger and his Secret Service agents said words to the effect of, "I guess we won't be telling Mrs. Clinton about this." Clinton replied, "Son, there's a lot of things we won't be telling Mrs. Clinton."

The second skit, and probably my favorite, was after Clinton survived the impeachment attempt. President Clinton, then played by the hilarious Darrel Hammond, slowly walked up to the presidential podium and said, "I . . . am . . . bulletproof. Next time, you best bring some kryptonite." It just made Clinton's legend ever stronger. Sometimes, when someone is attacked so much and survives so much, even if he deserve the negatives, everyone almost cheers for him or respects him as a survivor or even starts to pull for him because he is suddenly an underdog with everyone after him. The "I am bulletproof" line just summed up a feeling that Clinton would do whatever he wanted and get away with it. Hillary Clinton is the Secretary of State and potential future President. Bill Clinton is loved like crazy and will only become more loved as time passes and he continues to do post-Presidential efforts that are usually endearing and not controversial. Hillary is demonized and Bill is made even more lovable. Remember when Hillary went nuts when someone asked her what Bill Clinton thought about something instead of asking her what she thought as Secretary of State? The Clintons will bring us much more entertainment for years to come.

In October of 1998, Vice President Al Gore visited the City of Seven Hills to watch John Glenn blast off into space again at John Glenn Elementary School. The school named after Senator Glenn made for a perfect backdrop for the big space mission. When Gore first came on the scene, I thought he was great. He was talking about the environment and some other issues that were of interest to me. When I was in college, I wrote a column for *The Collegian* called "Earth Watch" and even way back then I was writing about recycling, planting trees, oil spills, adopting manatees, and other green issues.

Then, I lost interest in Gore because he was such a stiff when he would talk. Watching him debate George W. Bush was almost painful. Seriously, Al, you were the Vice President of the United States. Try to pull it together. Now, I find myself paying attention again to some of the things Gore has to say and a lot of people don't realize that he has made an incredible fortune since he left politics. I'm talking tens and tens of millions if not more.

I don't care who it is, when the Vice President comes to my tiny town, it is exciting. I respect the office no matter what. I was just a councilman at the time and at that Gore event, I witnessed arguably the dumbest thing ever done by any elected official – EVER! I won't say the guy's name because I know his daughter and she is nice and probably embarrassed enough by this story, but no joking - we had a long-term councilman who can best be described as goofy. We'll call him Councilman Goofy for the rest of the story.

Mind you, this was the Vice President visiting so there were dozens of people in the press corps following him and in attendance. It was all staged in advance; elementary students would ask the Vice President pre-determined questions about space, and John Glenn, and a bunch of other happy topics. The Vice President and astronauts from Cleveland's NASA Research Center would answer them. One of the questions was, "What was the shortest flight in space?" The correct answer given by a student was Alan Shepard on Mercury 3. It was at this moment when something compelled Councilman Goofy to interrupt and correct the Vice President of the United States and say, "That's wrong. The shortest flight in space was by the Challenger."

I could hear the gasps of the entire crowd, like they had just been punched in the gut. I remember burying my head in my hands hoping no one would take a picture that showed me sitting near this guy. To his credit, Vice President Gore looked at this fool and calmly said, "Yes, thank you for reminding

Vice President Al Gore gives a look of disbelief at the dumbest comment in history.

us of that terrible tragedy. We must never forget their great sacrifice . . . blah, blah, blah." The whole time Gore was trying to spin this fumble he was looking at Councilman Goofy like, "Are you serious? You seriously just said that?" The look on his face was priceless and I captured it in my photo.

I met then-candidate George W. Bush at Burke Lakefront Airport. Cleveland has this stupid airport that occupies prime Lake Erie real estate. When I go to Chicago and see what that city has done with its lakefront, I want to beat up our city planners when I think about Cleveland's wasted opportunity. Cleveland's lakefront has a shipping port, Cleveland Browns Stadium (used about 10 times a year) and this giant airport that services rich people flying their little corporate jets. The majority of the water is cut-off from pedestrian access by a giant highway. This is the same highway that has a 90-degree right turn in it called "Dead-Man's Curve" because of the countless accidents that take place in the area. There is a highway in Cleveland that has drivers traveling due north at 65 miles an hour – and all of a sudden – they have to make a perfect, 90-degree right-hand turn. It's as if they were building the highway and realized they were getting close to Lake Erie, so they built in a right turn - on a HIGHWAY!!!! As if driving on Cleveland's icy roads in January isn't fun enough, these geniuses thought they should put in some more adventure and kill people. Why stop there? Why doesn't the city install land mines that people have to drive through or how about missing bridges that people have to clear like the *Dukes of Hazzard*?

Bush landed in a private jet seating about 10, gave a quick talk, and then greeted about 200 people in line. He was upbeat and friendly and posed for pictures. One of the keys to having a successful meet and greet is having someone with you who has a clue and knows how to take a picture. I was shaking Bush's hand and getting an autograph. While he was signing, I looked back at my friend behind me and posed for my picture with the future President. My friend gave me the "thumbs up" that he got the picture. Of course, when I got the pictures developed, my dumb friend had zoomed in on just Bush. I'm not even in the picture. When I talked to him, he said, "Oh, I just thought you wanted a picture of Bush?" No, Einstein, I wanted to be IN the picture with Bush. Really, are people this stupid? If you ever want a close-up of just the top of Bush's head, I have it.

A great moment for Bush was when he threw out the Ceremonial First Pitch in Game Three of the 2001 World Series at Yankee Stadium. This was right after the September 11th tragedy and, like a matador, Bush walked to the center of Yankee Stadium wearing a New York Fire Department fleece with a bullet-proof vest underneath, wound up from the top of the pitcher's mound, and fired a perfect strike to the catcher. The place went crazy with chants of U-S-A, U-S-A!

I know this is very difficult to do because the first time I threw out a first pitch as mayor, I almost killed someone. We had Seven Hills Night at Jacobs Field with the Cleveland Indians. Nearly 1,000 people from Seven Hills bought discounted tickets to the game and as a reward I got to throw out the ceremonial first pitch. I have played baseball since I could walk. I have successfully played every position on the field including pitcher. In my youth, I usually had the strongest arm on the team. Of course, I often usually had the wildest arm on the team. One time I was playing shortstop in high school and I fired a throw to first base into the stands, causing fans to dive for cover. My favorite player growing up was Julio Franco and like him, I would throw from every angle imaginable. My natural throw was this angry side-arm motion and I can't tell you how many base-runners' heads I almost took off while trying to complete a double-play throw to first base.

The day of the game, I went up to Valleywood Park at lunchtime with my friend, John Link. It was summer so I was in baseball mode and my arm

President George W. Bush signing an autograph for Mayor David Bentkowski. You cannot see the Mayor because his friend is a dumb ass that didn't get him in the picture.

felt great. It was so much fun practicing that afternoon. My arm felt great and I must have thrown 50 pitches to John as practice. I was firing the ball like I was Roger Clemens. I thought my first-pitch debut would be a piece of cake. I was "popping" John's glove. I kept saying to myself, "Whatever you do, make sure you throw it the whole way and do not bounce it." Throwing out the first pitch is a losing proposition. It sounds fun, but it is not. If you throw a strike, you might get a few claps. If you throw a ball, you will get booed emphatically. The payoff for the risk is just not worth it.

They announced my name and all of my fans and voters were in one section of the park and they went crazy cheering for me. The field announcer joked about me having a fan club. As I was standing on the pitcher's mound, I realized it was also Cleveland Clinic night and on the field were a bunch of cancer survivors. The good news was they survived cancer. The bad news was the Indians had them lined up standing behind the catcher and home plate. As I was about to fire a rocket to the catcher, I suddenly saw all these cute grannies with grey hair standing way too close for comfort to the catcher.

I immediately panicked and didn't know what to do. Did you ever see those carnival games where you throw the ball and try to knock over the clowns for a prize? That nightmare was my reality. I was thinking to myself, "If I fire a ball and I overthrow it, chances are I am going to strike and kill a cancer survivor." I don't know much about polling, but I'm pretty sure that is a good way to ruin my approval rating. I thought, "I'll side-arm it so it

Mayor David Bentkowski takes the mound at Jacob's Field to throw out the Ceremonial First Pitch.

stays low and if I hit someone, at least it will be their leg and not their little fragile, peanut-skull." I went into my windup and fired the ball to then Indians player Ben Broussard. The ball barely – and I mean barely – cleared the grass and bounced in the dirt about five feet in front of Broussard. I still have the ball and it still has the red dirt mark on it. He lunged for the ball on his knees just trying to keep it from hitting anyone. In all of my years of going to Indians' games, I have never heard such a loud "boo." I wanted to tackle the mascot, Slider, and steal and put on his costume so no one saw me.

The Indians have good beer at their games and by the time I made it back to my Seven Hills section, most of my friends were pretty liquored. If you are a young guy and you have young guy friends, all joking and teasing is fair game. Within seconds of walking into the section, friends like Jeff Philips and Tim Maffo were standing up heckling me and laughing. I had no choice but to play along and let everyone have their fun. The throw was that bad; there was no defending it. One of my sweet grannies said to me, "Just stick to being mayor, honey. Baseball is not your thing." OUCH!!!!

Mayor David Bentkowski with the classy First Lady Laura Bush.

The following year the Indians invited me back and I told everyone, including the Indians, I don't care if a dozen nuns are standing behind home plate, I am throwing the ball as hard as I can and I don't care who I hit. Sure enough, I walked out there . . . did a full wind-up and leg kick . . . and fired a bullet right down Main Street. About three people clapped, two of whom were my parents.

Bush walked out to the center of Yankee Stadium right after we were attacked and said, "Come on, you terrorists, come and get me" and he fired a strike wearing all that extra gear. I'm not sure he should have even done it because if he would have made a throw like my first one, we would have looked wimpy to the world. Thankfully, with one pitch, Bush gave us our swagger back.

As a mayor, the list of political dignitaries I have met is long. Some are such important figures that they at least need mentioning including First Lady Laura Bush (classy), Congressman John Kasich (great guy), Ohio Governor Bob Taft (nerdy), Secretary of State Condoleezza Rice (intimidating and a Browns fan), Ohio Senator George Voinovich (short), Ohio Senator Mike DeWine (shorter), Congressman Dennis Kucinich (shortest), and the Reverend Jesse Jackson.

For years, I have done a Jesse Jackson impersonation similar to the one Darrell Hammond did on *Saturday Night Live*. No matter how hard I was trying, when I met Jesse Jackson, every now and then while talking to him I would slip into my impersonation voice. I didn't even want to keep talking to him because I knew I was doing it but there was no one else around and I talked to him for about five minutes. "I had . . . trepidation . . . about

"What's up, my brother?" Mayor David Bentkowski learns black handshakes from the Reverend Jesse Jackson.

our . . . conversation . . . as I conducted . . . a . . . mutilation . . . of my . . . word . . . presentation." The other funny thing is Jesse Jackson gave me the black guy handshake and hug. It was a sweet thought, but again, I'm from Seven Hills. I had no idea how to reciprocate. When white guys meet other white guys, we shake hands and say, "Hi, Larry, I'm David." When I met Jesse Jackson, it was like the "hand-jive" scene out of *Grease*. I didn't know what the heck was happening. At least I didn't ask him who Malcolm "10" was.

Elected officials and public servants have good days and bad days. Think about it, when is the last time your local newspaper or television news did a favorable story about an elected official? The fact is that the vast majority of people who serve never have the hint of scandal. I always tell people I am interested in helping the same way a guy who wants to coach little league or someone who volunteers at church wants to help. Our system of government is the greatest in the world and I worry that if we continue to abuse our officials who don't deserve it, we are discouraging future generations from wanting to serve their country. Remember, we are government "of the people" and "by the people." The saying is not going to hold true if no one wants the job because it is not worth putting up with the personal attacks. I know it sounds like a losing concept, but we need good people to go run for their local city council, and get involved. Echo my words and help me try to convince people that public service is an honorable thing to do.

So Who Is Next? You!

I'm at over 71,000 words and the people who have to edit this book are not happy about it. In case you haven't noticed, I like to write a lot! Writing all these stories has been easy for me because I am just rehashing events that happened to me and how I remember them.

The big question the whole time I have been writing this has been, "How does the book end?" I have a lot of life to live hopefully. I plan on giving more proclamations in the future. And, best of all, I promise that if this book is a hit and I make some good money with it, I will go find even crazier adventures and tell you all about them. I am term-limited as mayor. I need to figure out what happens next in life.

Given all that, I think the best way to end the book is to talk about who I want to meet next. If tens of thousands of people read this book, chances are there will be people who read it who can help make those future meet and greets happen for me. If I haven't said it enough already, I am thankful to everyone who took the time to meet me. Seriously, I'm just a young guy from Seven Hills, and the fact that so many people gave a hoot about meeting me does mean a lot. I still think they were all crazy and were duped into thinking I was important, but hey, give me a tip of the hat for being creative and help me see what else I can hustle.

The most important people I want to meet going forward are not celebrities, but hopefully the tens of thousands of people I am going to meet on my cross-country book tour. I love America and I love to travel. Supposedly, this book will be printed and released on November 4, 2009. On that date, I am loading up my car with hundreds of books and I am going to drive across the country promoting my book and my city. If I end up on Howard Stern's or Martha Stewart's show, you bet I am going to plug Seven Hills and tell everyone how great it is.

When I do the book tour, I plan on meeting and speaking everywhere I can. My first trip, I will head through Pennsylvania, work my way to Massachusetts, visit Rhode Island and Connecticut, spend a week in New York and New Jersey, and then work my way back to Ohio through Philadelphia, Pittsburgh, and a bunch of colleges. It is going to be a blast. After that trip, I will spend some time visiting the South . . . and the Midwest . . . and the West . . . and anywhere else people will have me.

I am going to visit old dudes at Rotary meetings, I am going to talk to business people at chamber of commerce luncheons, and I am going to party with students on campus. Each day, I will talk to as many radio, newspaper and television people as possible. Each day, I will meet with city officials from the cities I visit and pick their brains for useful ideas. I have decided that something has called me to write this book, and more important, something is calling me to tour the country and see what happens.

Of course, I hope to sell enough books to pay for this learning experience. Also, who knows, maybe enough crazy stories will take place on these trips to allow me to write a second book. But the big thing is I want to meet tons of people and learn from them. I want to grow as a person, celebrate others, and figure out new ways to help my community. If you hear I am coming to town, come see me and give me a story. Give me an idea. Give me a memorable encounter. Give me free tickets to the Penn State/Ohio State football game. Whatever - your guess as to what happens next is as good as mine. Let's figure it out together.

Don't get too excited. You are probably not going to get a proclamation when you meet me. But, here are some people I would like to give proclamations to in the future:

President Barack Obama – I have never given any President a proclamation and it would be my great honor to do so because I have tremendous respect for the Office. Can you imagine me in the Oval Office giving the President a proclamation? I think it would send a great message. I voted for McCain based on his record of service, but as I said, "Once Obama was elected, he is my President and I want him to do well for my country." The President entertaining me would send a great message about rewarding a young man who has already spent nearly 15 years of his life in public service.

It would help send a message that if someone is involved in government and service, exciting things like meeting the President can still happen. I am an advocate for young people, the environment, volunteerism, and patriotism. I deserve to meet the President more than some dumb athlete who wins a sports championship. Let's make it happen.

Jack Nicholson, Leo DiCaprio and Gene Hackman – For as long as I can remember these have been my three favorite Hollywood actors. Jack and Gene are movie royalty and have been in so many great movies I would need more chapters to name them. Leo is the best actor of his generation and I dig how he conducts himself. I don't just want to meet these guys; I want to have an adventure with them. I want to sit next to Jack and watch the Cleveland Cavaliers battle the Los Angeles Lakers. I want people back home to flip on their televisions and say, "What the heck is Bentkowski doing sitting next to Jack Nicholson?" I want Leo DiCaprio to take me backstage to a Victoria's Secret fashion show and say, "Adrianna, I want you to meet my friend, David." Actors and celebrities have agents and press people who are always trying to generate publicity. Trust me, if Leo DiCaprio takes me backstage to a Victoria's Secret show, I will make sure the whole world knows about it. Come on, guys, think of something fun for us and let's go do it. Other actors who would be cool meeting would include Will Farrell, Tom Cruise, Tom Hanks, Johnny Depp, Brandon Routh, Heather Locklear, Larry David, Jerry Seinfeld, Brad Pitt, Bill Murray, Vince Vaughan, Owen and Luke Wilson, Ben Stiller, Rebecca Jarvis, David Letterman and Regis Philbin.

Jim and Kim Neumeyer, David Eppstein, Ed and Tanya Bittman, Pete and Lisa Draganic, Heather Greenaway, Peter Wendell, Gary Suhadolnik, Darren and Hannah Mieskoski, and Nicole Pratt - These are all people I have known over the years who have been special to me above and beyond everyone else for various reasons. Jim and Kim Neumeyer are my dear friends from college. The day they moved into their new house, they mailed me a key and said "Come stay anytime you want." I was in their wedding, Jim and I were college roommates, and Kim used to let me keep Jim out dancing until 3:00 a.m. at Frankie's. I love them very much.

David Eppstein was my best friend in law school and is hilarious. I have a funny story about David. We once drove Yehuda's equipment all the way to South Miami Beach for a concert. Once we unloaded the equipment, the giant, empty cargo van was our "wheels" for a few days in South Beach. David and I were lying on the beach and by some miracle three gorgeous models from Australia came and asked to tan with us. They had just arrived in the country and were doing photo shoots. When it was time to go, the girls needed a ride and we offered to drive them back to their hotel. It didn't dawn on me that we were driving the van until we started walking up to it taking up three spots on the street. Without hesitation, these three girls hopped into the back of the van and it didn't even have seats, just a blanket on the floor. David and I just looked at each other like, "Doesn't this seem weird and creepy to you?" We were cracking up. As we closed the van door, I was waiting for scary music to start in the background. Once in the van, I said, "Girls, do us a favor. Don't ever accept a ride from strangers driving an empty cargo van in the future. It's probably not a good idea." They had no idea how it could be dangerous and after I told them there was an awkward silence as they were probably thinking "Did he tell us not to get into a cargo van because he is a crazy killer?" If I wouldn't have been such a noble guy and not scared them to death with my worrying and parenting, this could have been a good story with a happy ending.

Gary Suhadolnik was a former State Senator for Ohio and the guy who taught me most of what I know about campaigning and running for office. I was just a 23-year-old kid when I was first elected and Gary spent night after night knocking on doors with me, asking his donors to send me donations, and securing me yard sign locations. He's happily retired and I don't get to see him too much anymore, but he played a major role in my political life.

I could go on and on about dozens of people like this but you get the idea. They were and are important to me and I wanted to mention them.

Oprah Winfrey – "Dear Oprah, I have spent nearly 15 years of my life doing public service. I could be a multi-millionaire if I took all of that time and effort and put it towards my business. I could be a super-rich lawyer. I could have lobbying offices across the country. Instead, I chose to help my home of Seven Hills and sacrificed insane amounts of money. Please let me meet you on your show, give you a proclamation, and then you can tell everyone to go buy my book. If ever someone should be rich, it should be me because it is in my nature to just dump the money back into public service and helping others. I don't need fancy cars or clothes. I'm a frugal Pollack. Remember, I used to buy my suits at Value City. Help me become super rich and I promise I will continue to lead a life of charity and try and use my money to help others. Your pal, David"

Julian Stanczak is the master of Op Art, an art movement that was named after his first exhibit in New York. Growing up in Seven Hills, I lived just two houses away from him. His son, Christopher, and I played Matchbox cars together just feet away from him as he painted priceless creations. His talent is just ridiculous. He manipulates color and uses squares and other figures to create movement. One look at his paintings and they seem like they are alive or moving. I knew he was a big deal, but I'm not an artsy kind of guy, so that world is foreign to me. I was in New York once and I walked up to the snobby curator lady in the gallery and said, "Excuse me, Miss, do you know who Julian Stanczak is?" Really smugly she said, "Everyone knows who Julian Stanczak is!" The guy has paintings across the globe. He has painted the outsides of buildings. He is just an amazing talent and an amazing story. He survived the Holocaust. I love him because he is a gentleman and he's Polish. Julian and his wife, Barbara, also a famous sculptor on her own, have lived in Seven Hills for many decades on my parents' street, and they even allowed our rec. center to hang up a bunch of his prints. Imagine visiting some city rec. center, and there were gorgeous Stanczak paintings hanging on the wall. It was awesome.

Beck, Garbage, Depeche Mode, New Order, Jimmy Buffett, Chris Isaak, Coldplay, U2, Billy Joel, Neil Diamond, Engelbert Humperdinck, Roberta Flack, Brittany Spears, Prince, REM, the Violent Femmes, the Smashing Pumpkins, The Cure, the Beastie Boys, Lenny Kravitz, the White Stripes, Madonna, and Norah Jones – Some of these I have tried to meet and failed like Beck, Garbage and Depeche Mode. Others, I realize, I probably have no chance of meeting, like U2. Hey, Bono, forget about that Nobel Prize, how about a proclamation? Others are legendary figures who would probably cause me to have a heart attack if I met them, like Madonna and Prince. What they all have in common is that I am a huge fan of theirs. Oh, and I want to meet Norah Jones again to see if she really thought I was cute.

Senator John McCain – I have talked about it a couple times, but I feel this man is an amazing American hero and I simply want to meet him to thank him for his service to our country. He exemplifies how we should all feel and act in regard to these United States.

Calvin Klein – If it weren't for Calvin Klein, all of this might not have ever happened. When I went away to college, I only had saved up enough money from working at Denny's to pay for my first quarter of school. I had no plan and no cash in the bank. The first day of school, I went to the local mall and was walking through Hudson's. A guy behind the fragrance counter called me over, and said, "Don't take this wrong way, but you are a good looking guy and the Calvin Klein rep was just here and they want me to find some college guy to be their new fragrance model." I'm like, "Heck, no, I'm not spraying perfume." He said, "It's $14 an hour and your job is to flirt with girls, and get them to buy Calvin Klein cologne for their men." "SOLD – you had me at $14 an hour." For the next three years, and then for a couple years back in Cleveland, I was the perfume guy in the mall. If it wasn't for that job, chances are I would not have been able to stay in college. Isn't it amazing how one person or one event can change a life?

The job was the greatest. My regional boss, Judy Belanger, was so cool. I love her to this day and still keep in touch. She would constantly be sending me free Calvin Klein stuff. She had so much of this product; she sent it to me to get it out of her house. I had cases and cases of this stuff and came up with creative promotions to get rid of it. Ironically, I love Calvin Klein not only because that job changed my life, but if I were a famous celebrity, his stuff is all I would wear. I love the way his clothes look. They look classic and stylish. In my mind, that is how suits and shirts and other clothes should look. Back then, his colognes were the best. Obsession, Eternity, Escape, CK One – they sold themselves. I loved that job so much and worked hard at it because I knew I was lucky to have it. I started getting my friends like Jim and Kim Neumeyer perfume jobs as well. I would be in the mall spraying Eternity and Kim would walk by and spray me with Tiffany or Aramis. We all sold like crazy and we all made extra dough.

Judy Belanger is another person who made a major impact in my life. She stuck up for me and made sure I kept that job and taught me so much about marketing. When I worked for Calvin Klein, even as a fragrance model, I was exposed to his marketing genius and I received all kinds of training. I learned more about marketing from working for Calvin Klein than someone could learn in ten college marketing courses.

When I went for the job, after I met Judy, they flew me out to Chicago to meet a woman named Kathy Cullen. I remember this story like it was yesterday and I still keep in touch with Judy and Kathy and I have laughed about it with them on several occasions. I was 18 at the time and I met Kathy in a gorgeous hotel lobby. I was sitting there in a suit that was way too big for me. The fancy hotel lobby had these giant sliding doors. I was sitting there waiting, and all of a sudden, the sliding doors opened and standing like a vision was Kathy Cullen. I have no idea what she looks like now, but back then, she was stunning. She looked like a Calvin Klein model, even though she was some big shot vice president. She had on a dark blue suit that looked like something Christy Turlington would wear. She walked over to me with this sultry walk, extended her hand, and in a sexy voice said, "Hi, I'm Kathy Cullen." I took her hand, and the only thing I could think to say was, "Hi, I'm in love." I was so nervous, I almost wet my pants. I just kept talking and talking. Kathy was great and she gave me the job. She probably figured I would talk people to death unless they bought and she was right. I was a sales wizard.

John McEnroe, Derek Jeter, Joe Montana, Andy Roddick, Anna Kornikova, Andrea Agassi, Wayne Gretzky, Roger Clemens, Nolan Ryan, World B. Free, Julius Erving, Larry Bird, Michael Jordan and Sugar Ray Leonard - These are some of my all-time favorite athletes and I have a million questions for them.

Colin Jennison, Wade Brennan, Alex Jennison and Gerry Strother – I met these guys in Cleveland but want to party with them in the future because they are destined for stardom. They are a tribute band that plays The Killers and Coldplay and they blew me away with their talent, especially lead singer Colin. We paid $12 to see them and I would pay $100 the next time. They were that good. I met them after the show. Colin is in his early twenties. I said something to him about money, and he said something sincere along the lines of "I'd be happy to play for free. This is so much fun I just love to do it." That is a great attitude, kid, but don't sell yourself short. You are extremely talented and I want to be in on the ground floor because I know you can be huge.

Finally, I'll end this book by stating some day when I die, I will be very happy to meet again my grandmother, Mollie. Grandma and my mother, Barbara, are the two greatest women to ever have lived. I love them both so much I can't even begin to explain to you what they mean to me.

I have a beautiful story about my grandmother that would be great for the movie I have been threatening to write for many years. The story about my grandmother I am about to tell you is completely true, which makes it so amazing. I was born in the 1970s on December 23, just two days before Christmas. I was the apple of everyone's eye, especially my mother and my grandmother. My grandmother gave me a yellow, smiley-faced pillow that first Christmas and there is a picture of me next to it under the tree. Apparently, as a baby, I loved that pillow, and of course, loved being held by grandma. Although I am sure she loved all the grandkids equally, everyone agrees that we had a special relationship and I was even the person chosen to give her eulogy.

As I got older, no one ever knew what happened to that pillow. I was first elected to city council in 1995, and my grandmother did get to see me get sworn in although she had the beginnings of dementia and would have good days and bad days. Years later, I was running for office again, and the same day we finally had to put my grandmother in the nursing home, it was also the day I had to decide what to put on my campaign signs. They had to go to the printer for the November election. The day we put my grandmother in the nursing home, I was going through old photos looking for pictures of her to put up on her wall at the nursing home.

While going through the photo albums, I found the picture of me as a baby with the smiley pillow. The idea hit me like a ton of bricks. I would put a smiley-face on my campaign signs because as I campaigned in the summer heat, the signs would remind me of my grandma, and it would encourage me to keep pushing. In addition, I always wanted to be a positive, clean campaigner and I didn't want to be in nasty elections. The smiley-signs were my way of saying, "I'm here to talk about my ideas and not be a nasty opponent."

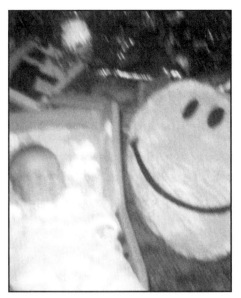

Mayor David Bentkowski with his special smiley pillow given to him by Grandma Mollie.

At this time, my grandmother had fairly advanced Alzheimer's and her mind just wasn't normal. There is no way she would have comprehended my use of the smiley-face logo. I knocked on thousands of doors that summer carrying my smiley-face sign and everyone loved it.

One interesting thing I learned when I would visit her is the bizarre way Alzheimer's affects people. In nursing homes across the world, senior citizens might not remember their names or their loved ones' names, but in a cruel trick, their minds let them remember certain things from their past. A lot of nursing homes have entertainers come in and sing for the seniors. I have seen senior citizens that couldn't remember their own name but can sing and know every word to "Battle Hymn of the Republic" or "God Bless America." It's as if certain things are stored somewhere in the memory and they come out with no rhyme or reason. In addition to patriotic songs, go to any nursing home in the country, and chances are you will see seniors sing "You Are My Sunshine." This song was one of my grandma's favorites, and remains one of mine because of her.

My grandmother passed away and it was devastating. She had lived in some old house in Cleveland but because of ethnic pride, never wanted to move. The house had an upstairs that no one had been in for years. We were afraid we would fall through the floor, it was so old. After my grandmother died, my parents went to the house to check it one last time to make sure there weren't any keepsakes. They went upstairs into an old room and were getting rid of various items. They came across a giant bag hanging in a closet.

My dad is the impatient type and just wanted to throw everything away and be done with it. My mom said, "Wait a minute. This bag is wrapped secure. Whatever is in here, she wanted to protect it." My parents opened up the bag and it was the original smiley-pillow. For decades, grandma kept that pillow because it reminded her of me and make no mistake about it, I will protect it and keep it for the rest of my life.

I have used the smiley-face on my campaign signs for many elections. Grandma wasn't alive to see me elected mayor, but I know she would be proud of me. On any given Election Day, I'll stand outside the polls holding my campaign sign and throughout the day, I will look at that smiley-face and the Heavens and think of her. I know she is always with me.

One day, I found in a store a smiley-face magnet that when the nose is pushed, it plays "You Are My Sunshine." My grandma was buried in a mausoleum and I put this smiley button on her burial stone. The curator once told me that every now and then, someone would push the button and the song would play. It is comforting to think that my sunshine might hear her song and know she is still in my heart.

I didn't want this book to be about all the things I have done for Seven Hills because that is self-serving. However, I don't want everyone to think all I do is try to meet celebrities and wonder how I stay elected. I am blessed to have been re-elected with 82 per cent of the vote; just trust my people of Seven Hills and know that I work hard and smart for them. The book is meant to be that fun side of me that I have earned by working hard for my community. I believe one individual can make a difference. There is a reason *It's a Wonderful Life* is my favorite movie.

If you want to know more about my service and accomplishment record, I am sure there is stuff out there you can find. However, just to give you a flavor, there are a few things that I am proud of that I'll quickly mention so you don't think I'm a total screwball.

I was one of the first people in the country to bring up the potential dangers of camera phones in private places like lockers and showers and contacted Congressman Mike Oxley's office about implementing some protections for people and he did. In Seven Hills, we have led the state of Ohio in using a new form of concrete paving where workers grind off portions of an old concrete road and put new concrete on top of it. We call it "white-topping" and we have successfully paved over 20 streets in this new manner and they are proving to be a home run that has saved the city hundreds of thousands of dollars. Every week, we receive calls from other cities asking us how to do it.

As mayor, I pushed for Seven Hills to be one of the first to use the automated blue recycling carts. We gave 5,200 houses in the city a free 35-gallon container and we have a recycling participation rate of about 85 per cent. I'm a "green" guy, so this was a no brainer and the reduction in the trash stream has saved us hundreds of thousands of dollars. We do other cool green measures such as accept used motor oil and cleanly burn it to heat our service garage. We provide rain barrels, mulching mower blades, and have had rain garden demonstrations to help the environment. We have eliminated hundreds of septic tank systems and fixed improper cross-connections that were causing storm-water contamination. We have eliminated most paper at City Hall and have routine hazardous material round-ups for paint cans, tires, batteries, et al.

Crime incidents in the city are virtually nonexistent and we have made the city even safer by adding manpower to the firehouse, adding a K-9 unit and computers in all police cars, and by making sure all safety forces have the best equipment such as bulletproof vests and oxygen tanks. We even have oxygen masks for dogs and cats so the firefighters can save pets in a fire. Seven Hills is that awesome! Big crime news occurs if kids knock over a granny's mailbox.

We have done great on budget items and were in the black in 2008 despite this terrible economy. Cities around us are laying-off dozens of people, issuing furloughs, and cutting services. We're just fine in Seven Hills and will be in great shape when the economy improves.

I am always looking for improved commercial development and we have positioned our city with a developer to build a 75-acre, $375 million lifestyle center. It has been talked about for 30 years and I was able to assist a developer in finally acquiring all the needed land. When I showed up at people's kitchen tables and told them they should sell, they trusted me and believed in me, and we made it happen. I showed them how they could invest a $500,000 guaranteed offer and how quickly it would equal their $600,000 initial asking price.

Using a special fund and not money from the general fund, we just spent nearly $400,000 giving every street in the city a new street sign. They look amazing and they were the next step in our beautification puzzle where we have painted all fire hydrants, bought new street sweepers, removed any graffiti or out-of-date items, etc. Next on the agenda is a $1.5 million streetscape project for our main business district including red brick fronts, new curbs, sidewalks and aprons, 250 symmetrically spaced trees, flowers, banners, and a lighted archway with the city script. It's going to look "pimp."

I am big on technology and we have completely revamped our website, have added city videos that we email to people, have a computerized phone system that sends updates immediately to every house, and, of course, yours truly remains available to anyone who calls at his home phone number of 216.901.0269. That's right, in Seven Hills, the whole town, and now you, have the mayor's home phone number. Please respect this generous gesture and do not call me at 4:00 a.m. You can also "friend" me on Facebook or join my Facebook fan page.

We like to party in Seven Hills and we have created a yearly calendar of city events that have grown into "big deals." Our Home Days festival is the biggest around with two nights of fireworks and over a dozen bands. Other community favorites include a Harvest Festival and Chili Cook-off, an Opening Day for the little league with 1,000 kids, and a Christmas celebration with our VFW post.

You get the idea; I have made this job my life and I have loved every minute of it. Seven Hills is truly "God's Country, USA," and those who live here love it more each day. It is truly my great honor to be the Mayor of Seven Hills. I want to thank my loving voters who have made it possible.

I hope they are proud of the energy and ideas I brought to them and our city. I'm confident my grandma would be and that is usually my yardstick for judging my actions.

Grandma, this book and all of my public service is for you.

Instead of typing "The End," I am more of a "This is just the beginning... and I'll see you real soon" kind of guy.

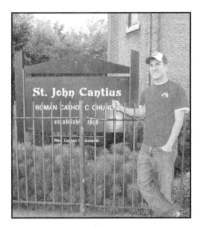